The Life of Irony
and the Ethics of Belief

SUNY Series in Philosophy
George R. Lucas, Jr., editor

The
Life of Irony
and the
Ethics of Belief

David Wisdo

STATE UNIVERSITY OF NEW YORK PRESS

Published by
State University of New York Press, Albany

©1993 State University of New York

All rights reserved

Printed in the United States of America

For information, address State University of New York
Press, State University Plaza, Albany, N.Y., 12246

Production by Cathleen Collins
Marketing by Theresa A. Swierzowski

Library of Congress Cataloging in Publication Data

Wisdo, David, 1957–
     The life of irony and the ethics of belief / David Wisdo.
         p.   cm. — (SUNY Series in philosophy)
     Includes bibliographical references and index.
     ISBN 0-7914-1221-0 (hard) : — ISBN 0-7914-1222-9 (pbk.)
     1. Religion—Philosophy.   2. Irony.   3. Conduct of life.
I. Title.   II. Title: Ethics of belief.   III. Series.
BL51.W63   1992   91-38202
121'.6—dc20   CIP

10   9   8   7   6   5   4   3   2   1

FOR LAURIE

In grown-up philosophy, the problems we have *remain* answerable only through growth, not through explanations or definitions. The idea of growth is meant to emphasize that we are no longer to expect answers and solutions in traditional terms—any more than we can accept philosophical questions and answers as *given*.

Stanley Cavell
from *Themes Out of School*

Contents

Acknowledgments / *ix*

1. Self-Trust and the Ethics of Belief / *1*

2. The Ethics of Belief and Personal Knowledge / *13*

3. The Ethics of Belief and the Meaning of Life / *37*

4. Religious Belief and Self-Understanding / *55*

5. Self-Deception and the Ethics of Belief / *73*

6. The Fragility of Faith / *87*

7. Reductionism and the Ethics of Belief / *105*

8. Between Objectivity and Subjectivity: The Life of Irony / *127*

Bibliography / *141*

Index / *149*

— Acknowledgments —

E ven if every book does not tell a story, every book surely has one. This book's first incarnation took shape between 1987 and 1989 during my appointment as a Henry R. Luce Post-Doctoral Fellow at the Divinity School of Yale University where I had the opportunity to explore many of these ideas in my seminar on the "Ethics of Belief." I would like to thank the students enrolled in that course, as well as the faculty and administration for their encouragement and support for this project. In particular, I would like to thank David Kelsey who read an earlier version of the manuscript and provided thoughtful criticisms and comments. Others at Yale who provided inspiration and encouragement in a more informal way include Louis Dupre, George Lindbeck, Gene Outka, Margaret Farley, Richard Fern, Kathryn Tanner, and the late Hans Frei. Finally, I would be remiss if I failed to mention that many of these ideas were initially developed during "coffee hour" discussions with Russell Reno, who took a special interest in many of these questions. I am especially grateful for his thoughtful conversation and companionship.

I would also like to thank my teachers, particularly Wayne Proudfoot and Scott Davis, both of whom helped me shape and define many of the issues discussed here. As my advisor and mentor at Columbia University, Wayne Proudfoot has been a model of careful scholarship and has provided thoughtful guidance and encouragement on this project as well as others. Scott Davis has proven to be an endless source of peripatetic wisdom, and for this I am truly grateful. In addition, I would like to express my appreciation for the support and comments provided by James Wetzel, Edward Mooney, and Gordon Marino, all of whom have taught me much about the virtues and pleasures of thoughtful conversation.

The final incarnation of the manuscript took shape at Susquehanna University where I have had the privilege to hold the Weber Chair in the Humanities for the past two years. I would like to thank both the administration for providing me with this opportunity and my colleagues in the Philosophy and Religion Department for their encouragement.

Brief sections of two chapters appear elsewhere in a slightly different form. Part of Chapter 5 appears as "Self-Deception and the Ethics of Belief," in the *Journal for Value Inquiry*, October 1991, and is reproduced here with the permission of Kluwer Academic Publishers. Part of Chapter 6 appears as "The Fragility of Faith: Toward a Critique of Reformed Epistemology" in *Religious Studies*, September 1988, and is reproduced here with permission of Cambridge University Press.

Finally, I want to thank my family, especially Laurie, for her patience, love, and editorial common sense, and Emily and Alexander, who, in their childhood wisdom, would rather play with their toys.

— *1* —

Self-Trust and the Ethics of Belief

> Men seem to be constitutionally believers and unbelievers.
> There is no bridge that can cross from a mind in one state to a
> mind in the other. All my opinions, affections, whimsies, are
> tinged with belief,—incline to that side. All that is generous,
> elegant, rich, wise, looks that way. But I cannot give reasons to
> a person of a different persuasion that are adequate to the force
> of my conviction. Yet when I fail to find the reason, my faith is
> not less. . . .
>
> *Ralph Waldo Emerson*[1]

Worries about whether or not we can defend our deepest and most cherished beliefs need not arise solely because of our inability to make ourselves understood by those who demand some kind of justification of our views. Although people may find it almost impossible to render an account of their convictions that will satisfy the challenges of others, they may still find that their faith remains unshaken and undisturbed. In the journal entry cited above, for example, written in 1833 during his first excursion to Europe, Ralph Waldo Emerson celebrates his unqualified confidence by noting that the strength of his faith does not depend on his ability to make himself understood by everyone. Like his Danish contemporary Søren Kierkegaard, Emerson is well aware that there are limits to our ability to defend and justify our basic concerns and convictions and that true inwardness demands courage as well as a willingness to take the risk of "becoming subjective." Acknowledging what often seems to be the unbridgeable chasm that separates believers from nonbelievers, Emerson voices what is clearly a Kierkegaardian

1

insight concerning the difficulty of making the basis for one's religious beliefs intelligible to others.

It is tempting, of course, to view Emerson's observation about the impossibility of meeting such challenges to one's beliefs as an apologetic ploy that might enable him to ignore or dismiss the claims of others who might demand a stricter standard of intellectual accountability. The suspicion is that his remarks concerning the limits of argument might actually be nothing more than a subtle rationalization intended to forestall any criticism of his own views. For if the believer and unbeliever discover that they cannot understand the force of each other's convictions, reasoned debate would seem to be impossible: one's beliefs would not be vulnerable to the challenges of those who did not share one's views. If Emerson is right, then believers would appear to have no reason to fear that an inability to defend or justify their religious convictions might lead to the erosion or loss of their faith.

Emerson, however, is obviously no apologist and expresses throughout his writings a firsthand knowledge of the vulnerability of religious belief. In fact, what at first appears to be the expression of an optimistic and naive confidence is actually the hard-won result of his own struggle with religious doubt.[2] From the crisis of 1832, when he begins to express strong doubts about the Lord's Supper, to the end of his life, Emerson wrestles with meaning of faith as he attempts to come to terms with the changes and transformations in his own religious beliefs.

In the world according to Emerson then, the most difficult and formidable challenge to a person's faith is not the demand for some kind of justification that might be acceptable to everyone—worries concerning the fragility of faith do not arise primarily as a reaction to one's failure to justify one's beliefs to others. Rather, the crisis that renders belief vulnerable is the discovery that one's basic beliefs no longer make any sense in the context of one's life viewed as a whole.

For Emerson then the ethics of belief is not primarily a question of whether people are able or willing to justify their beliefs to others, but is rather a matter of cultivating what he calls the virtue of self-trust. The ideal of "Man Thinking," for instance, which he articulates in his well-known address "The American Scholar," provides us with a paradigm of the kind of person for whom inquiry is a matter of subjective reflection, a matter of the heart. This does not mean, of course, that self-trust is an ideal that excludes any reference to intellectual accountability. On the contrary, Emerson's ideal of "Man Thinking" portrayed in "The American Scholar" is akin to Friedrich Nietzsche's "free spirits" whose vocation demands the almost impossible ability to balance self-trust with an austere suspicion of themselves and their beliefs:

Long he must stammer in his speech; often forgo the living for the dead. Worse yet, he must accept—how often! poverty and solitude. For the ease and pleasure of treading the old road, accepting the fashions, the education, the religion of society, he takes the cross of making his own, and, of course, the self-accusation, the faint heart, the frequent uncertainty and loss of time which are the nettles and tangling vines in the way of the self-relying and self-directed. . . .[3]

Self-trust then does not necessarily entail a blind dogmatism or a stubborn refusal to assess critically one's way of life. Quite the contrary, there is a sense in which the virtue of self-trust is based on an unconditional desire for truthfulness and a willingness to sacrifice security for a life of discovery. In short, self-trust should not be confused with intellectual complacency. It is, rather, a demanding task pursued in solitude: "In silence, in steadiness, in severe abstraction, let him hold by himself; add observation to observation, patient of neglect, patient of reproach; and bide his own time,—happy enough if he can satisfy himself alone that his day he has seen something truly."[4]

On the one hand then Emerson recognizes that a meaningful human life requires a certain practical self-confidence. This claim is based on the fact that it is difficult if not impossible to sustain our faith in our life projects unless we are willing to *claim* them as projects for which we are willing to assume responsibility.[5] By the same token, however, Emerson is suspicious of those who ensure the stability of their beliefs and commitments by espousing a kind of "existential" dogmatism. The problem with such strategies is that they are motivated by a desire to render one's particular worldview invulnerable to any challenge. The result is an inability to entertain or acknowledge new life-possibilities. The kind of practical self-trust that Emerson recommends throughout his writings requires the cultivation of a mean between confidence in one's own commitments and the insights of a moderate skepticism. In short, the ethics of belief is a matter of balancing self-trust and creative flexibility, for it is only by virtue of our practical self-confidence that we can acknowledge without fear strange and unfamiliar ways of thinking about life:

> Keep the habit of the observer, and, as fast as you can, break off your association with your personality and identify yourself with the Universe. Be a football to time and chance, the more kicks, the better, so that you inspect the whole game and know its uttermost law. As true is this ethics for trivial as for calamitous days.[6]

As this short passage from Emerson's journal indicates, one of the ways we might articulate the notion of self-trust is to speak of keeping the *habit* of the observer, a habit that requires a willingness to be challenged by the unexpected and unfamiliar: to "be a football" to time and chance. This remark is important to the extent that Emerson characterizes inquiry not in terms of some method or theory of human understanding that might insure knowledge but rather in terms of a certain kind of habit that might enable one to balance practical self-confidence with a willingness to explore new ideas. The assumption underlying this Emersonian insight, an insight I shall explore and defend throughout this essay, is that genuine inquiry depends not on our ability to formulate or defend a theory of knowledge, but on the cultivation of a certain kind of character and style of thinking.

The value of Emerson's remarks on inquiry is the suggestion that the ethics of belief is not primarily an epistemological concern. Like the later Heidegger, who invites us to turn our attention from the traditional philosophical preoccupation with the problem of *knowledge* and reappropriate instead the more original notion of *thinking*, Emerson advocates a more holistic picture of philosophy and insists that *thinking* must involve serious reflection about ordinary life. Rejecting the traditional views of those philosophers and theologians for whom the ethics of belief is primarily a problem of the *justification* of religious *knowledge*, Emerson emphasizes what his contemporary Kierkegaard calls edification and insists that spiritual inquiry is primarily a matter of the way we *understand* our life-views and *appropriate* them by claiming them as ours.

In order to appreciate the radical implications of a proposal such as that offered by Emerson or Kierkegaard, we need only remind ourselves of the extent to which both call into question the traditional picture of inquiry dating back to Descartes and Locke. According to this traditional approach, the ethics of belief has generally been cast as an epistemological issue. Thus, the question of whether a person is entitled to hold a religious belief has, until recently, been regarded as a question of whether the position can be justified or defended by the application of some reliable and universally accepted method. As we shall see in the next chapter, the paradigmatic example of this approach can be found in the work of John Locke, whose *Essay Concerning Human Understanding* sets the agenda for the development of the ethics of belief by framing the problem of religious belief as an epistemological worry.

It was not long though before this narrow characterization of the ethics of belief set forth in the work of Locke began to elicit critical responses from those who saw his epistemological project as a threat to religious belief. Since the development of this debate among Locke's immediate contemporaries has been explored in detail elsewhere,[7] I will examine the responses of two later figures who attempt to broaden the terms of the debate. In particular, I am interested in the way thinkers such as Samuel Taylor Coleridge and John Henry Newman rethink the problem of the ethics of belief by seriously considering the *personal* component of religious belief often overlooked by Locke and his followers. As we shall see, both thinkers give us good reason to be wary of any approach to the ethics of belief that ignores or systematically discounts the complex ways that personal considerations about the purpose of life figure into the reasons one might have for one's religious beliefs.

After a brief discussion of Coleridge and Newman it will come as no surprise that I intend to defend throughout the remainder of this book the view that the ethics of belief is not primarily an epistemological concern but rather an issue of character and critical self-reflection. In the third chapter we shall see that it is just this insight that informs the work of Ludwig Wittgenstein, who wants to rethink the ethics of belief in such a way as to avoid the problems raised by traditional formulations of the issue. Much, of course, has been written about Wittgenstein's views on religion and it would be impossible to do justice to all of the controversial issues raised by his work. My focus will be much more narrow and will involve the simple thesis that religious beliefs should not be construed as isolated claims but rather as holistic interpretations about the meaning of life that enable us to make sense of our emotions and desires as well as our attitudes about suffering and death.

Although it might appear to make little difference whether we view a person's religious convictions as involving certain judgments about the meaning of life, there are important consequences in construing religious beliefs in this fashion. For example, it is impossible to assess such life-views in any straightforward way with respect to their "plain truth" because our practical deliberations about life's meaning are, as David Wiggins claims, "cognitively underdetermined."[8] This notion of "cognitive underdetermination" is important because it suggests that our views about the meaning of life differ in at least one important respect from scientific theories. In short, although our judgments about life's meaning involve an attempt to make sense of certain "existential data" such as love, suffering, and death, we do *not* expect our judgments about the meaning of life to converge in the same way that we expect our scientific theories to converge. In other words, Wiggins's account suggests that it is simply a mistake to suppose that there might be a single interpretation of life that is "true" by virtue of the way the world is. In the end then even though discussion about the question of the meaning of life has become unfashionable in some philosophical and theological circles,[9] we cannot avoid the conclusion that if religious beliefs involve judgments about life's meaning, and if such judgments fall short of plain truth, then religious beliefs also fall short of plain truth.

Now although such a conclusion might appear to be a liability, it is, upon closer examination, a liberating and fruitful suggestion. For one thing, once we acknowledge the connection between the ethics of belief and a person's basic questions about the meaning of life, we will be in a better position to grant the extent to which our religious convictions are tied to the way that we understand ourselves in light of our fundamental commitments and projects. Since there are limits to a purely formal discussion of this issue, I will try to elucidate this claim in the fourth chapter by drawing upon literary works, including Leo Tolstoy's *Anna Karenina*, that might illuminate in a more concrete fashion how the ethics of belief is tied to a person's attempt to come to some self-understanding about the meaning of life. Most importantly, by attending to the way such issues are explored in literature, we shall discover that the criteria for assessing a person's particular interpretation about life's meaning have more in common with the aesthetic criteria we employ to understand characters in a novel than they do with the impersonal epistemological criteria to which many philosophers of religion appeal in their attempt to assess the intelligibility and defensibility of a person's religious beliefs.

Once we grant the importance of more flexible criteria for the assessment of a person's beliefs, we will also be in a better position to understand how the pursuit of practical self-understanding shapes and authorizes a person's religious beliefs. On the one hand, some thinkers, such as Søren Kierkegaard, have suggested that there are important connections between the cultivation of faith and self-examination. Now while this Socratic approach provides a helpful model for understanding the dynamics of the life of faith, we might still wonder whether a person's religious commitments might place certain limits and constraints on the forms this pursuit of self-understanding might take. One might ask, for example, whether it is the case that the pursuit of self-understanding can sometimes put a person's faith at risk. Is it the case that certain forms of self-reflection, such as psychoanalysis, might serve to challenge and even undermine the stability of a person's religious convictions by offering alternative possibilities for making sense of life? And if this is a possibility, could one make the case that it is appropriate to draw practical limits to either the type or scope of self-inquiry in order to avoid placing one's particular religious identity at risk? These are just a few of the issues that a reexamination of the ethics of belief might help us understand.

Another closely related problem is the issue of self-deception: both the case of theists who are self-deceived in their faith as well as atheists, such as Ivan Karamazov, who might be said to be deceived in their unbelief. Since I will explore this topic in more detail later on, I will just mention two aspects of the problem here. First, any attempt to do justice to the ethics of belief must be willing to consider whether a consideration of self-deception should be a factor in assessing religious belief. Such an inquiry is complex since it is still an open question whether self-deception is *always* epistemically or morally blameworthy. But if it turns out to be the case that self-deception is sometimes blameworthy, it would appear to be an important consideration in assessing a person's religious convictions. Second, it seems clear that the only way to do justice to this type of concern is to move in the direction that I am proposing and to explore what it might mean to assess one's religious beliefs in terms of one's character as a whole.

Of course, once we begin to take these considerations into account, we will also be able to make better sense of what it means for a person to lose faith. Unfortunately, many contemporary philosophers of religion who rightly criticize Locke's foundationalism and evidentialism as well as the ethics of belief they entail still present an overly reductionistic picture of religious belief that distorts the dynamics of the religious life. In particular, thinkers such as Alvin Plantinga and the many others who defend what has come to be known as "reformed epistemology" fail to give sufficient attention to the many ways one's loss of faith might be tied to changes in one's most fundamental concerns and interests. Very often, one's loss of faith should be interpreted not so much in epistemic terms, but rather in terms of the erosion of those basic cares and concerns that constitute one's identity as a believer. The problem is that even when "reformed epistemologists" do attempt to account for the loss of faith, they often succumb to the temptation of accounting for this loss of belief in terms of "sin." Unfortunately, this strategy fails to do justice to the perspective of the person in question who would most likely reject such appeals to the notion of sin in favor of a more naturalistic explanation for this loss of faith. Once again, I shall maintain that any attempt to do justice to the ethics of belief must account for this kind of story.

There are, of course, many ways a person's faith can be put at risk, but one of the perennial challenges to the believer's religious convictions has been the problem of evil. Traditionally, the religious skeptic has posed the question by asking how an omniscient, omnipotent, and benevolent God could permit the existence of natural and moral evil. At first glance, such a challenge would appear to pose a serious threat to the integrity of the believer's convictions. More specifically, the atheist's suggestion is that anyone who acknowledges the seriousness of evil but continues to believe in God is basically irrational. We shall see though that it is a mistake to construe the concern in these terms. The question of whether belief in God is compatible with the existence of evil is not primarily a question of whether theism is or is not rational or logically coherent. Instead, the problem of evil presents an *ethical* concern and the only way to do justice to this issue is to explore how our responses to evil reflect the shape of our characters as a whole.

In order to show what might be gained from regarding the problem of evil in ethical terms rather than as a problem concerning the rationality of religious belief, I will characterize several possible responses. On the one hand, theists who manage to maintain their faith in the face of evil must be wary of succumbing to the vice of blindness. Part of the problem is that it is all too easy to evade the difficulties posed by the existence of evil by appealing to theodicies and other facile philosophical solutions. But even if one eschews the temptations of such reductionistic theodicies and opts for more modest means of dealing with the problem, such as the Free Will Defense proposed by Alvin Plantinga, one still runs the risk of rationalizing an unacceptable response to the problem.

Of course, it is important to stress that the theist is not the only one susceptible to vice when it comes to the problem of evil. The atheist must also be on guard against succumbing to what can be called the vice of defiance. The classic example of this type of response is Dostoyevski's famous character Ivan Karamazov, for whom the problem of evil raises what appear to be insurmountable worries and difficulties. Unlike the theist who appeals to theodicy at the risk of being blinded to evil, the atheist, such as Ivan Karamazov, runs the danger of appealing to the existence of evil as an excuse for avoiding responsibility for it. But such defiance is no less blameworthy than the blindness of those believers who fail to appreciate the many ways that the acknowledgment of evil and suffering might challenge one's Christian self-understanding and lead to the erosion of a person's religious beliefs.

If the problem of evil is not basically a problem about the rationality of religious belief, it is rather an ethical concern—a concern about the kind of people we want to be and about the best ways to respond to this problem. We shall discover that the best way to avoid the twin vices of blindness and defiance is to cultivate what Simone Weil would call the virtue of attention. What is needed, says Weil, is a respect for reality of the world, a willingness to accept the extent to which our identities and all that we hold to be important can be put at risk by evil and suffering. The proper response to the challenge posed by the existence of evil is the cultivation of a kind of loving attention that would allow us to acknowledge the vulnerability of what is most precious to us. Of course, the price for this kind of realism is high. For once the individual acknowledges the possibility of such vulnerability, there is nothing that might not be lost, including a person's faith.

After considering the fragility of faith in terms of how the existence of evil and suffering can challenge and in some cases undermine a person's religious beliefs, I will take up what has come to be known as the problem of reductionism and religious belief. Unfortunately, the debate surrounding the issue of reductionism has traditionally been motivated by epistemological worries concerning such issues as rationality and relativism. Some thinkers, such as D. Z. Phillips and Peter Winch, are wary of social scientific approaches to the study of religion on the grounds that such attempts misdescribe and distort what the believer actually believes. On the other hand, critics of Phillips and Winch, such as Wayne Proudfoot, maintain that such worries about reductionism usually conceal tacit apologetic concerns and that what is necessary is a more subtle analysis of reductionism amenable to social scientific approaches to the study of religion.

Although there may be some merit in treating reductionism as a worry about rationality and relativism, I will argue in the penultimate chapter of this book that these concerns have no direct bearing on the problem of the ethics of belief. If we want to make sense of why certain people find religious reductionism to be objectionable, it is better to think of such objections as ethical ones, in the broad sense of that term. If, for example, we examine the work of Ludwig Wittgenstein, who addresses this issue in writings such as "Remarks on Frazer's *The Golden Bough*," we will discover that his argument against reductionism in religious studies is primarily a moral one. What Wittgenstein finds objectionable about such "scientistic" views is not simply that they distort the data by misconstruing or misdescribing particular religious beliefs, doctrines, and practices; rather, the threat is that such approaches will blind us to the importance of religion for human life and that a failure to see that there is something "deep" in religion can lead to a spiritually impoverished life.

In the final pages of this book I turn to some recent considerations of the problem and suggest that the life of intellectual virtue is a life that manages to maintain the precarious and difficult balance between objectivity and subjectivity. Unlike many rationalistic philosophers of religion who search in vain for some abstract canon of rationality or some methodical way of thinking about our lives that might ensure our confidence in our basic beliefs and commitments, I will argue for a more radical but liberating proposal. Appealing once again to the work of Ralph Waldo Emerson, I will suggest that our ability to maintain self-trust without succumbing to the temptation of dogmatism depends on a particular *style* of thinking that balances subjectivity and objectivity. Since there is no decision procedure that might enable us to avoid the vices of dogmatism or skepticism, we must rely on a kind of practical confidence governed by openness and flexibility, a style of thinking one might call "Emersonian pragmatism."

At first glance, it might seem that this kind of proposal is a blatant concession to intellectual chaos and irrationality. This is not the case. As Richard Rorty has recently suggested, this kind of *ironic* attitude toward one's beliefs is a natural and acceptable part of modern liberal culture.[10] Following Rorty I will conclude that the ethics of belief is not an epistemological issue at all but primarily a matter of our willingness to cultivate the *style* of thinking that characterizes what he calls "the liberal ironist."[11]

In the end, I would like this reflection on the ethics of belief to help us better understand the limits of argument. My thesis, I believe, is deceptively simple and involves the claim that our failure to reach agreement in our judgments about religion and the meaning of life is not a failure of rationality but is rooted in the limits of what we are willing to acknowledge with respect to commitments and concerns we may not share. Grounds for such disagreements are inevitably self-involving and are tied to the many different ways we understand ourselves in light of our basic commitments. My claim is simply that we can make better sense of what it means to carry on such discussions if we rethink the debate in terms of the model of the ethics of belief that I am proposing here. To say that there is much to be gained from regarding the ethics of belief primarily in terms of intellectual character and critical self-reflection concerning our basic projects and commitments is not to guarantee some formula to help us reach some sort of agreement. On the contrary, it is perhaps the only way to understand why believers and nonbelievers so often fail to agree and why the one thing needed is a renewed commitment to the virtue of tolerance.

Notes

1. *Selections from Ralph Waldo Emerson*, ed. Stephen E. Whicher (Boston: Houghton Mifflin Company, 1957), pp. 15–16.

2. I reject the standard stereotypical reading of Emerson that reduces him to a naively optimistic idealist. It will become clear throughout this book that I want to propose and defend a picture of Emerson as a pragmatist whose optimism is tempered by an acknowledgment that optimism is a difficult achievement. In this respect, my reading of Emerson draws upon the insights of Stephen Whicher's classic study *Freedom and Fate: An Inner Life of Ralph Waldo Emerson* (Philadelphia: University of

Pennsylvania Press, 1953). For discussions of the "pragmatic" strain in Emerson's thought, see Frederic Ives Carpenter, *Emerson Handbook* (New York: Hendricks House, Inc., 1953), esp. pp. 164–78, as well as his essay "William James and Emerson" in *On Emerson*, ed. Edwin Cady and Louis Budd (Durham: Duke University Press, 1988), pp. 43–61. The best discussion of Emerson's pragmatism is Cornel West's "The Emersonian Prehistory of American Pragmatism," in *The American Evasion of Philosophy* (Madison: University of Wisconsin Press, 1989), pp. 9–41.

3. Ralph Waldo Emerson, *Nature, Addresses, and Lectures*, intro. Robert E. Spiller (Cambridge: Harvard University Press, 1979), p. 62.

4. Ibid., p. 63.

5. This line of interpretation draws on Stanley Cavell's insightful reading of Emerson. See especially *In Quest of the Ordinary: Lines of Skepticism and Romanticism* (Chicago: University of Chicago Press, 1988), *This New Yet Unapproachable America: Lectures after Emerson after Wittgenstein* (Albuquerque: Living Batch Press, 1989), and his recent Carus lectures *Conditions Handsome and Unhandsome: Emerson's Constitution of Perfectionism* (Chicago: University of Chicago Press, 1990). Cavell's reading and appropriation of Emerson's writings is explored in Russell Goodman's interesting book *American Philosophy and the Romantic Tradition* (Cambridge: Cambridge University Press, 1990).

6. *Selections from Ralph Waldo Emerson*, p. 81.

7. For an excellent discussion of the impact of Locke's epistemological project on the religious thought of his day, see John W. Yolton, *John Locke and the Way of Ideas* (Oxford: Oxford University Press, 1956).

8. See David Wiggins, "Truth, Invention and the Meaning of Life," in *Needs, Values, Truth* (Oxford: Basil Blackwell, 1987), pp. 87–137.

9. Recently, however, some philosophers have expressed a renewed interest in this topic. See, for example, Oswald Hanfling, *The Quest for Meaning* (Oxford: Basil Blackwell, 1988); John Kekes, *The Examined Life* (Lewisburg: Bucknell University Press, 1988); and Robert Nozick, *The Examined Life: Philosophical Meditations* (New York: Simon and Schuster, 1989).

10. The position I defend in this book is inspired by Richard Rorty's *Contingency, Irony and Solidarity* (Cambridge: Cambridge University Press, 1989).

11. Rorty develops this line of thinking in "Private Irony and Liberal Hope," in *Contingency Irony, and Solidarity*, pp. 73–95.

2

The Ethics of Belief
and Personal Knowledge

The modern system of philosophy has one great advantage,
which makes it difficult to attack it, with any hope of success,
namely, that it is not founded on any of the prevailing opinions
or natural feelings of mankind. It rests upon a single principle—
its boasted superiority over all prejudice. Unsupported by facts
or reason, it is by this circumstance alone enabled to trample
upon every dictate of the understanding or feeling of the heart,
as weak and vulgar prejudices. In this alone it is secure and
invulnerable. To this it owes its giant power and dreaded name.

William Hazlitt[1]

A. *The Legacy of Descartes and Locke*

It has become something of a commonplace among secular-minded
critics of religious belief that one is not entitled to believe in God unless one can offer some kind of proof or evidence to support this claim.
Moreover, there is often a tacit assumption that a failure to provide evidence in support of one's religious views is not simply a cognitive or intellectual failure, but a moral one as well. Underlying the debate between
the theist and atheist is an assumption that belief in God is morally
blameworthy unless theists are ready to defend their position by appealing to objective reasons which are acceptable to everyone. What makes
such an assumption so problematic is the Enlightenment claim that
there might be some neutral epistemological framework which provides
the context for settling these kinds of disagreements. According to this

way of construing the ethics of belief, the believer and the nonbeliever who refuse to submit their beliefs to the arbitration of this kind of impartial court can be taken to task for governing their beliefs in an irresponsible fashion. The problem is that even though there are good reasons to grant that there is an ethics of belief, such traditional attempts to articulate this issue as an epistemological concern often fail to do justice to the question by overlooking the extent to which the ethics of belief is primarily a question of *personal* knowledge.

The search for a reliable and impartial way of adjudicating competing knowledge claims begins with the worries expressed by René Descartes in his semi-autobiographical treatise, *Discourse on Method* (1637). In "Part One" of the *Discourse* Descartes makes the interesting and important claim that reason is a human capacity that all people share. Unlike some philosophers who sometimes seem to suggest that reason and intelligence are the prized possessions of a privileged few, Descartes expresses confidence that everyone is capable of thinking for themselves. But if this is true, wonders Descartes, why is it the case that different people come to different conclusions about the same issues? In other words, once we accept an egalitarian view of reason, we must first account for the fact that people hold a wide variety of opinions concerning religion, morality, and science and then try to adjudicate among the competing claims by formulating some way to discover the truth of the matter.

As we read through the *Discourse*, it soon becomes clear that Descartes is perplexed and deeply troubled by these differences of belief. If someone, such as himself, is interested in finding answers to these most important questions, where should one begin? In a narrative that amounts to something like "a portrait of the philosopher as a young man," Descartes characterizes his pursuit of truth as a kind of quest. He begins, for example, by studying the works of the most "learned" scholars and philosophers. Unfortunately, he is soon disappointed to discover that the so-called learned philosophers cannot even agree with each other on these important questions and that they have little to offer a young inquiring mind. In the end, he concludes that the only thing we can learn from the scholars is how ignorant we really are: "I found myself beset by so many doubts and errors that I came to think I had gained nothing from my attempts to become educated but increasing recognition of my ignorance."[2]

Descartes's assessment of the epistemic chaos of his day begins with a consideration of theology, concerning which he confesses that although he "aspired as much as anyone else to reach heaven"[3] he could not understand it. Next, he examines the writings of the philosophers only to discover that these intelligent people cannot come to any agreement about the most important questions of human life. In fact, it becomes clear to him that the diversity of conflicting philosophical views can only serve to undermine our confidence in our ability to find the truth. Descartes recognizes that there are other sciences, but examines them only to conclude that "nothing solid could have been built upon such shaky foundations."[4] Finally, to make matters worse, Descartes notes the despair the seeker after truth is likely to experience as he contends with the claims of pseudosciences ranging from astrology and alchemy to magic. Not surprisingly, the young Descartes comes to suspect that the world of ideas is nothing more than a realm of confusion.

How does Descartes respond to this confusing situation? In "Part One" of the *Discourse*, he confesses that he decides to close his books and abandon the life of scholarship. This does *not* mean, however, that Descartes gives up his quest for knowledge. As it turns out, he hopes that what he could not find in the solitude of his study might be found in real-life experience. He travels throughout Europe, meets many interesting people, and hopes that common life might provide some answers to his questions:

> Resolving to seek no knowledge other than that which could be found in myself or else in the great book of the world, I spent the rest of my youth travelling,. . . testing myself in the situations which fortune offered me, and at all times reflecting upon whatever came my way so as to derive some profit from it. For it seemed to me that much more truth could be found in the reasonings which a man makes concerning matters that concern him than in those which some scholar makes in his study about speculative matters.[5]

What, however, does Descartes learn from his travels in the real world? Unfortunately, he is disappointed to learn that disagreement and confusion are not the exclusive characteristics of the learned scholars and that ordinary people have a wide variety of different customs and opinions. Once again, this diversity of opinions and different ways of life undermines Descartes's confidence and leads him to doubt all the things that he has come to believe on the basis of tradition and custom. In the end, what begins as a hope that real-life experience might dispel his perplexity ends up as the despair of more doubt and confusion.

How does Descartes respond to this perplexing situation? On the face of it, the temptation to abandon the search for knowledge would seem to be overwhelming. For this reason, it comes as no surprise that many of Descartes's contemporaries opted for this kind of "solution" by becoming skeptics. As Richard Popkin argues in his classic study, *The History of Scepticism from Erasmus to Spinoza*,[6] the skeptical response to epistemic crisis of the sixteenth century gathers momentum with the discovery of the writings of Sextus Empiricus, a second-century philosopher whose work became widely available when it was published in 1562. According to Popkin, the rediscovery of Sextus Empiricus was especially important for religious thinkers such as Michel Montaigne (1533–92) who argue that skepticism can actually be a source of solace and consolation to those who suffer from moral and religious doubts. Skeptical fideists such as Montaigne claim that once we abandon the futile and fruitless search for truth, we can devote our attention to more profitable projects. This does *not* mean, however, that we should give up our moral and religious beliefs. According to the fideist, we should simply accept these beliefs on faith.

What is Descartes's reaction to this skeptical solution to the problem? As we read the *Discourse*, it becomes clear that he *rejects* it. Unlike those skeptics who despair and abandon the quest for truth, Descartes decides to devote the rest of his life searching for an alternative. And what is Descartes's solution? As we read the *Discourse* we learn that the only alternative to skepticism is the discovery of a reliable *method* that might ensure our ability to acquire certain knowledge:

> I say without hesitation that I consider myself very fortunate to have happened upon certain paths in my youth which led me to considerations and maxims from which I formed a method whereby, it seems to me, I can increase my knowledge gradually and raise it little by little to the highest point allowed by the mediocrity of my mind and the short duration of my life.[7]

How then might one begin to formulate a method that might enable a person to acquire certain knowledge? Descartes suggests that we should begin by examining those methods which do in fact seem to yield this kind of knowledge and ask whether we can extend the principles that govern these methods to other areas. Descartes is especially impressed by the impartiality of disciplines such as mathematics and geometry that seem to command universal agreement and expresses his hope that these disciplines might provide a paradigm for his project. Not surprisingly, the goal that Descartes pursues throughout the rest of his career is the formulation of a rationalist system that justifies itself on the basis of several self-evident truths concerning the nature and existence of God and the self.

It is important to remember that the attempt to formulate a framework for deciding religious questions is not limited to rationalist thinkers such as Descartes. Perhaps the most well-known attempt to articulate the ethics of religious belief by appealing to a neutral epistemological framework can be found in the work of the empiricist John

Locke (1632–1704) whose *Essay Concerning Human Understanding* (1689) provides us with the most ambitious project of this type. The position developed by Locke, which commonly goes by the name of evidentialism, has come under attack in recent years, but it is important to remember that the concern that motivates the position appears to be a legitimate one. For if it is permissable to believe something on insufficient evidence, one might ask, as John Locke does, how we are to distinguish the well-founded religious convictions of the responsible believer from the mere prejudice of enthusiasts who claim to base their privileged knowledge of God on some private experience or intuition? More specifically, Locke wants to insist that if our goal is knowledge, it is blameworthy to settle for either the blind opinion of the enthusiast or the innate ideas of the Cartesian. In order to do justice to this concern, Locke himself proposes an approach to religious knowledge and the ethics of belief that might help people to govern their religious convictions in a more responsible fashion.

Perhaps the most important thing to remember about Locke's philosophy of religion is that it reflects, like his philosophy as a whole, an assumption that inquiry is an activity that characterizes in an essential way what it means to be a human being. Even though it has become customary to invoke Locke's work as the standard foil for arguments against evidentialism and foundationalism, it is important to remember that his views concerning human understanding are informed by a strong commitment to what one might call certain "values of inquiry." More specifically, implicit in his discussion is the suggestion that rationality is a normative concept based on the presupposition that truth is a valuable thing that people ought to pursue. And although many might be tempted to say that Locke errs by presenting an overly intellectualist account of belief, we must not forget that his entire discussion about the nature and importance of inquiry presupposes that people should possess both a desire for truth and inclination to pursue it.[8] As he himself states at the beginning of his critique of religious enthusiasm: "He that would seriously set upon the search of Truth, ought in the first place to prepare his Mind with a Love of it. For he that Loves it not, will not take much Pains to get it. . . ."[9] Any discussion of human understanding must begin with the assumption that the cultivation of the mind is motivated by a love of truth.

The problem, however, is that although Locke believes that human inquiry should be motivated by a love for the truth, and that truth seekers should be able to reach some kind of agreement on the important questions of morality and religion, he is fully aware that we often fail to realize these ideals of inquiry. In the "Epistle to the Reader," for example, Locke recounts the kinds of concerns that originally led him to write the *Essay* in the first place and notes that he is especially troubled by the inability of people to engage in argument and inquiry in a methodical and orderly fashion. Indeed, it is interesting to note that even though Locke is extremely critical of the Cartesian rationalist who wants to settle such disagreements by an appeal to innate ideas, his project is motivated by worries and concerns that bear a strong resemblance to those voiced by Descartes in the *Discourse*. Consider, for instance, the following passage in which Locke expresses his frustration as he recalls one particular evening of conversation with his friends:

> Were it fit to trouble thee with the History of this Essay, I should tell thee that five or six Friends meeting at my Chamber, and discoursing on a Subject very remote from this, found themselves quickly at a stand, by the Difficulties that rose on every side. After we had a while puzzled our selves, without coming any nearer a Resolution of those doubts which perplexed us, it came into my Thoughts, that we took a wrong course; and that before we set our selves upon Enquiries of that Nature, it was necessary to examine our own Abilities, and see, what Objects our Understandings were, or were not fitted to deal with.[10]

According to this passage, the type of dilemma that motivates the entire project of the *Essay* can be spelled out in terms of the frustration we feel when the expectations that lead us to engage in debate and argument fail to yield knowledge. In order to highlight the problem, we might begin by noting the general assumption that people who engage in inquiry and debate do so because they are genuinely interested in acquiring a knowledge of the truth. In addition, we might make the more optimistic and perhaps more problematic assumption that knowledge is possible and therefore a reasonable goal for human beings to pursue. But if we grant these two rather commonplace assumptions, then the type of frustration that Locke expresses in the opening pages of the *Essay* presents us with a genuine dilemma. For if we assume that knowledge is possible, and that human beings who engage in conversation and argument do so in order to acquire such knowledge, then we need some explanation that might account for our failures to realize this goal. The hope, as Locke sees it, is that such an attempt to discover the reasons for our failures to acquire knowledge might also help us to identify some method or philosophical theory that could solve the problem and ensure the possibility of acquiring knowledge.

When we turn to the *Essay* to examine how Locke himself deals with this problem, it soon becomes clear that he offers two very different ways of answering this question that appear to be compatible on the surface but that mask an underlying tension running throughout his work.

In his more optimistic moments, Locke seems to suggest that the best way to facilitate inquiry and to realize the goal of knowledge is to discover some kind of neutral and reliable method that might enable us to reach this goal. According to this type of approach, people who gather in good faith to pursue knowledge fail because they have not undertaken the careful and painstaking analysis of knowledge and human understanding that Locke himself offers throughout the *Essay*. At times Locke appears confident that if we can manage to give a thoroughgoing account of understanding, we can rest assured that our inquiries will yield not blind opinion or prejudice, but true knowledge.

Locke's project therefore is motivated both by his concern over what often appears to be the intractable nature of moral and religious debate and by the hope that a neutral epistemological framework might ensure the possibility for settling such disagreements. In recent years, the significance of this kind of attempt to create a framework for the arbitration of moral and religious disagreement has been explored and criticized by several thinkers, most notably Alasdair MacIntyre and Jeffrey Stout. It is illuminating to note, for example, the similarity between Locke's approach to the ethics of belief and the account of rights criticized by Alasdair MacIntyre in his well-known study *After Virtue*.[11] According to MacIntyre, the history of moral thought since the Enlightenment can be characterized in terms of the erosion and fragmentation of our moral language and our increasing inability to settle moral questions. Although a detailed discussion of MacIntyre's subtle diagnosis of the present age is beyond the scope of this essay, it seems clear that he sees the language of rights and utility as ways of dealing with this problem. MacIntyre suggests that when the moral language of a tradition has deteriorated, the arbitration of conflicting moral claims will depend on our ability to discover some way to weigh and evaluate them, even if it involves the creation of what he would call a moral fiction. According to MacIntyre, the appeal to the notions of "rights" or "utility," which emerges as a response to this kind of problem, is just such an attempt to discover a neutral epistemological framework for the arbitration of moral conflict.

Those familiar with MacIntyre's work are well aware that he is rather pessimistic about these post-Enlightenment developments in moral thought. As his extended critique of the work of John Rawls demonstrates, MacIntyre himself has serious reservations concerning this "solution" to the problem of moral conflict and suggests that post-Enlightenment moral theories are at best unsuccessful attempts to cope with a rather desperate predicament.[12] The point I wish to make, however, is that MacIntyre's analysis of the motivations that underlie the appeal to such theories can help us better understand the concerns expressed by Locke in the *Essay*. More specifically, Locke's attempt to provide some neutral epistemological framework that might help us settle religious disputes is motivated by concerns strikingly similar to those that motivate the appeal to rights. Like the appeal to the language of rights, which is based on the assumption that there are neutral criteria for the arbitration of moral conflict, the ethics of belief debate emerges as the hope that a methodical analysis of the understanding might provide the epistemological key for settling religious debate. Moreover, like the appeal to rights, which requires a willingness on the part of all parties to suspend their own particular interests and to strive for some degree of impartiality, the ethics of religious belief, as spelled out by Locke, is based on the view that all religious knowledge must be based on objective and impersonal considerations. Appeals to personal considerations are ruled out by Locke because they are symptomatic of the kind of religious enthusiasm that is fundamentally inimical to methodical and orderly inquiry. In short, Locke's project seems to be motivated by the hope that a careful analysis of the understanding will help us settle religious debate and acquire true knowledge with a minimum of conflict in the same way that an appeal to rights might help us to settle moral questions.

As J. A. Passmore points out, however, there is a second, more pessimistic assessment of the problem found, for example, in Locke's critique of religious enthusiasm.[13] As already mentioned, Locke assumes that any account of human understanding must begin with the assumption that people have an inclination to seek the truth. The question we might ask, however, is whether this is a realistic assumption or whether it is the case that people are motivated by other inclinations that override their interest in acquiring knowledge. According to this way of addressing the problem, our failures to acquire knowledge are due not so much to a failure to provide a neutral and reliable method of conducting inquiry but are, rather, failures of character. Because we are motivated not only by a love of truth but also by a desire to believe what might make us happy, we are often victims of our own credulity. For this reason our desire for knowledge often leads not to truth, but rather to falsehood and illusion.

In a word, part of our predicament as lovers of truth is that the pursuit of knowledge is a fragile enterprise fraught with dangers. Locke suggests that our failure to acquire a knowledge of the truth can be explained in two rather different ways. As we have seen, if we assume that people are motivated by a love for the truth, and that knowledge is possible, we might be tempted to attribute our failures to the possibility that we might be ignorant of the true foundations of knowledge. In such a case, the solution is rather unproblematic and depends on our ability to give a technically reliable account of human understanding and to arrive at some type of reliable procedure for acquiring knowledge. However, at times Locke often suspects that not all failures to acquire knowledge are *epistemic* failures. Some failures are what we might call failures of character. Locke reminds us of the many ways we can be led astray in our pursuit of knowledge, not least of which is our desire to believe what makes us happy, rather than that which is true: *quod volumus, facile credemus*, as he quotes from Caesar.[14] Indeed, if Locke is preoccupied with a search for foundations, it is only because of an underlying anxiety that there is much that threatens our human, all too human, quest for knowledge.

Not surprisingly, Locke's philosophy of religion reflects a suspicion that, more often than not, our desire to alleviate our epistemological anxiety leads us to invent false or fictitious foundations for our religious claims. Those who seek refuge in religious enthusiasm or the Cartesian doctrine of innate ideas have achieved a kind of epistemological security—but at a price. Unfortunately, they have unwittingly adopted strategies that undermine their ability to revise critically their beliefs if they should happen to be false. The danger of appealing to such false foundations, claims Locke, is that they might tempt one to accept a belief as genuine knowledge even though it might turn out to be unfounded prejudice. The only legitimate response to this problem, concludes Locke, is to cultivate those virtues of inquiry that will enable us to revise our beliefs if they should happen to be false and to avoid both the vices of skepticism and dogmatism. In the final analysis then Locke has no doubt that the goal of inquiry is truth. The question, however, is whether there is any way to conduct our inquiries to ensure that we will in fact attain true beliefs and avoid false ones. As we turn to consider this issue, it will become clear that Locke's alleged evidentialism and foundationalism represent his response to this question.

According to Locke, the responsible Christian must first acknowledge the difference between those religious beliefs that are the object of certain knowledge and those that are a matter of probability, opinion, or faith. As it turns out, however, Locke argues that there is only one religious claim that is the object of certain knowledge; namely, the claim that God exists. Admittedly, such a bold claim might sound strange to the contemporary atheist who wants to argue that the belief "God exists" is at best a matter of opinion or faith. Locke, however, is confident that if there is anything about which the believer can be certain, it is the claim that God exists. But if, as Locke insists, the proposition "God exists" is not an innate principle, how can we be confident that it is true?

In order to answer this question we must briefly consider what Locke says about knowledge. First of all, Locke insists that after we distinguish between knowledge on the one hand, and probability, opinion, and faith on the other, we must recognize that there are different kinds of knowledge. The first type of knowledge, argues Locke, is what he calls intuitive knowledge. This fundamental type provides the necessary groundwork for Locke's epistemology to the extent that it consists of those self-evident principles that serve as the basic axioms of knowledge:

> For if we will reflect on our own ways of Thinking, we shall find, that sometimes the Mind perceives the Agreement or Disagreement of two *Ideas* immediately, by themselves, without the intervention of any other: And this, I think, we may call *intuitive Knowledge*.[15]

Like Descartes, Locke believes that intuitive knowledge is the most certain kind because it presents itself to the mind in the clearest light.[16] For example, the individual's apprehension of his or her own existence would be a paradigmatic case of intuitive knowledge. Locke is quick to point out, however, that although people have an intuitive knowledge of their own existence, it is impossible to have intuitive knowledge of religious claims such as the claim that God exists. Knowledge of God's existence, unlike knowledge of one's own existence, cannot be apprehended by merely inspecting the idea. Therefore, Locke needs to propose a second alternative:

> The next degree of Knowledge is, where the Mind perceives the Agreement or Disagreement of any *Ideas*, but not immediately. . . . Those intervening *Ideas* which serve to shew the Agreement of any two others, are called *Proofs*; and where the Agreement or Disagreement is by this means plainly and clearly perceived, it is called *Demonstration*.[17]

According to Locke, the claim that God exists is not a matter of intuitive knowledge but is rather an example of knowledge by demonstration. In this regard it is important to remember that demonstrative knowledge is no less certain than intuitive knowledge. So although it is not an axiom that God exists, the believer's conviction that God exists is defensible to the extent that he or she can give evidence to support this belief. Since the various premises of such a demonstration are themselves examples of intuitive knowledge, each of which is the object of certainty, the entire demonstration will preserve truth and thereby yield certain knowledge. Given this basic framework then, Locke attempts to construct such a demonstration in chapter 10 of book four in which he proposes a proof for God's existence. Beginning with a clarification of those self-evident principles that are derived from experience, Locke claims that we can rationally demonstrate that God exists and that the conclusion of such a proof yields certain knowledge.

Locke's empiricist approach to religious epistemology therefore begins with the assumption that the ethics of belief is primarily a question of whether a person can offer evidence to support his or her belief in specific religious propositions. For this reason, he wants to insist that people are not entitled to claim that they possess religious knowledge unless they are in a position to provide a convincing demonstration to show that God exists. Moreover, Locke seems to assume that the only way to carry out this demonstration in a responsible way is to begin with a kind of epistemological neutrality. The only axioms to which believers are entitled to appeal to defend their beliefs are those that would be acceptable to any reasonable person interested in whether the proposition "God exists" is true or false.

As many of his critics soon realized, however, it is far from clear that this narrow empiricist approach to religious epistemology can do justice to the personal dimension of a person's religious beliefs. Locke himself, of course, articulates the ethics of belief in these terms in order to undermine the claims of those religious enthusiasts who justify their convictions by appealing to innate ideas, intuitions, or some strange inner sense. However, even if we grant the legitimacy of Locke's concern, we might still ask whether his solution is defensible. As I have suggested, Locke maintains that the only way to deal with the problem of religious fanaticism is to base the ethics of belief on neutral epistemological considerations which exclude the individual's particular interests and concerns. One might wonder, however, whether this kind of approach to religious knowledge makes any sense at all. After all, what might it mean for a person to assume such a disinterested and neutral stance with respect to his or her beliefs? Is it reasonable to expect a person to defend his or her religious convictions without making any reference to the kinds of religious questions and interests that inform and shape these beliefs?

Traditional attempts to base the ethics of belief on neutral epistemological considerations are doomed to fail because we cannot even make sense of what it might mean to give a reason in this context. For this reason I intend to defend the views of Locke's many critics who wish to acknowledge the personal dimension of religious belief as a perfectly legitimate basis for giving reasons in support of one's convictions. After all, the reasons a person might offer to defend his or her belief in God might have little to do with objective and disinterested proofs such as the ontological, cosmological, or teleological arguments. More often than not, people are more likely to defend their religious convictions by appealing to what one might call, following the lead of Michael Polanyi, personal reasons.[18] One can imagine, for example, that people might tend to defend their religious beliefs solely in terms of their sense of sin and guilt and their need for salvation. Unfortunately, since Locke himself tends to be very suspicious of such sentiments to the extent that they tend to open the way for religious enthusiasm, he insists upon an austere and empirical approach to religious epistemology that leaves little room for these kinds of personal considerations. The question then is whether the possibility of religious enthusiasm warrants this rather extreme epistemological response or whether there is an acceptable way to incorporate personal considerations in our account of religious belief.

B. *The Romantic Response: Samuel Taylor Coleridge*

> In religious inquiry each of us can speak only for himself, and for himself he has a right to speak. His own experiences are enough for himself, but he cannot speak for others: he cannot lay down the law; he can only bring his own experiences to the common stock of psychological facts.
>
> *John Henry Newman*[19]

Given the constraints of Locke's program, it should come as no surprise why so many thinkers have expressed dissatisfaction with this approach and have explored alternative ways of construing the ethics of belief. Among the more well-known contemporary resources I have identified for rethinking this problem are thinkers such as Stanley Cavell, who appeals to the work of Ludwig Wittgenstein in an attempt to articulate the variety of ways "knowledge" is tied to our tacit commitments regarding our fundamental values and concerns. In the next chapter I will explore in more detail how these considerations can enrich our understanding of what it means to assess a person's religious convictions. What is interesting to note for our present purposes, however, is that even among earlier critics, the objections to Locke's position is often explicated in terms of his failure to acknowledge the personal dimension of religious understanding.

It was not long, for example, before many religious thinkers expressed their dissatisfaction with his narrowly empiricist approach to religious knowledge and suggested that it might be more helpful to explore the connection between religious knowledge and self-understanding. More often than not, however, the most thoughtful and insightful alternatives to such empiricist views of religious belief were offered not by philosophers, but rather by those thinkers of the Romantic tradition who found that poetic reflection might provide a way of rethinking in a radical way what had been traditional epistemological concerns. One of the more important and influential responses to the narrow approach to religious knowledge proposed by Locke and his successors is Samuel Taylor Coleridge's *Aids to Reflection* (1825)[20] in which he attempts to offer a more flexible account of belief that gives due consideration to the personal dimension of religious knowledge.

It is, of course, well known that Coleridge's early religious views were shaped and influenced in large part by those rationalistic philosophers who later became the target of his criticisms.[21] In his early work, for example, he appeals to the rationalistic views of David Hartley to defend his own version of determinism and draws from the work of thinkers such as Joseph Priestley to lend support to his unitarian beliefs. However, as J. Robert Barth points out, a variety of factors eventually led to the erosion of his rationalistic optimism,[22] and Coleridge came to realize that traditional accounts of religious knowledge could hardly do justice to his growing sense that religious beliefs must be tied to an individual's personal interests and concerns. In the end, such considerations led Coleridge to explore new ways of characterizing the activity of religious reflection in terms of self-knowledge. Consider, for example, the following observation taken from the preface of the work:

> READER!—You have been bred in a land abounding with men, able in arts, learning, and knowledges manifold, this man in one, this in another, few in many, none in all. But there is one art, of which every man should be master, the art of REFLECTION. If you are not a *thinking* man, to what purpose are you a *man* at all? In like manner, there is one knowledge, which is every man's interest and duty to acquire, namely, SELF-KNOWLEDGE: or to what end was man alone, of all animals, endued by the Creator with the faculty of *self-consciousness?*[23]

Like his contemporary Søren Kierkegaard, who has become well known for his notorious claim that "truth is subjectivity," Coleridge insists that it is a mistake to view Christianity as a theory or a philosophical system. Instead of seeking for some disinterested and objective reasons to ground or justify their faith, people seeking religious insight must begin by reflecting on their own interests and concerns. This Kierkegaardian insight is expressed in no uncertain terms when Coleridge remarks that "Christianity is not a Theory, or a Speculation; but a *Life;*—not a *Philosophy* of Life, but a Life and a Living Process."[24] For this reason, Coleridge presents his reader not with a speculative theological treatise but rather with a collection of aphorisms that may become the occasion for a kind of subjective reflection.

Unlike empiricists such as Locke, who maintains that religious knowledge is finally a question of *demonstration*, Coleridge is interested in developing a new way of articulating religious knowledge in terms of *edification*, to borrow once again a Kierkegaardian turn of phrase. In other words, Coleridge is sharply critical of those who characterize religious knowledge simply as a matter of whether people can defend or justify their beliefs by appealing to neutral epistemological considerations acceptable to everyone. Such a narrow rationalistic approach to the ethics of belief is a mistake, says Coleridge, because the *real* reasons why people hold certain religious beliefs are intimately connected to *personal* interests and concerns that cannot always be defended by appealing to objective considerations, that is, considerations acceptable to everyone.

Does this mean that such beliefs lack authority? Not at all. However, the only way to account for the *authority* that a religious belief has for people is by reference to the categorical interests of their conscience: "Revelation must have assured it, my Conscience required it—or in some way or other I must have an *interest* in this belief. It must *concern* me, as a moral and responsible Being."[25] As Coleridge sees it, the reasons a person might give for his or her religious convictions will always presuppose and include some reference to certain religious concerns and interests, such as a sense of guilt and a need of salvation, which *cannot* be characterized in nonreligious terms. It should therefore come as no surprise when Coleridge expresses his distrust of empiricist views of religious knowledge in very sharp terms:

> Hence, I more than fear, the prevailing taste for books of Natural Theology, Physico-Theology, Demonstrations of God from Nature, Evidences of Christianity and the like. *Evidences* of Christianity! I am weary of the word. Make a man feel the *want* of it; rouse him, if you can, to the self-knowledge of his *need* of it; and you may safely trust it to its own evidence.[26]

At this point we might ask how one can possibly make a person "feel the want" of Christianity. Coleridge, of course, is well aware that there is no direct way to convince a person that sin is the cause of our despair and that we all stand in need of salvation. Coleridge would agree that people do not come to characterize their lives in Christian terms as the result of some kind of demonstration. If a person does not feel the guilt of sin or the need for salvation, this is not the result of a failure to understand an argument: it is not simply an epistemic or cognitive failure. Such a failure, rather, is a failure of character, a failure that Coleridge's contemporary Kierkegaard calls "spiritlessness."

However, although argument plays no positive role in bringing a person to experience a sense of sin and a desire for salvation, argument may provide one means for removing those obstacles that prevent a person from coming to this realization. If, for example, we want to understand why many people do not acknowledge the reality of sin or fail to characterize their own sense of spiritual failure in these terms, we might begin by asking whether they really understand the significance of such Christian concepts as sin and salvation. In the "Introductory Aphorisms" at the beginning of the *Aids to Reflection*, Coleridge indicates that this is exactly the kind of concern that underlies his project. In the very first aphorism, he notes that the purpose of this work is to rescue truth from neglect by elucidating and clarifying those concepts that many take for granted:

> In philosophy equally as in poetry, it is the highest and most useful prerogative of genius to produce the strongest impressions of novelty, while it rescues admitted truths from the neglect caused by the very circumstance of their universal admission. Extremes meet. Truths, of all others the most aweful and interesting, are too often considered *so* true, that they lose all power of truth, and lie bed-ridden in the dormitory of the soul, side by side with the most despised and exploded errors.[27]

Once again it is difficult to resist the temptation of comparing the concerns expressed here by Coleridge with those voiced over and over again by his Danish contemporary Søren Kierkegaard. As already mentioned, Coleridge shares Kierkegaard's belief that a person's religious convictions presuppose certain religious interests and concerns, such as an interest in an eternal happiness, and that if one does not already have these interests, it is not likely one will acquire them as the result of argument or demonstration. There are simply no epistemologically neutral considerations that might bring a person to grant the importance and significance of Christian concepts such as sin and redemption. However, both Coleridge and Kierkegaard acknowledge and endorse the importance of clearing away the obstacles that might prevent a person from what Kierkegaard would call the "subjective appropriation" of these notions. In particular, both thinkers are especially concerned with the way Christian concepts lose their meaning and significance for people when it is assumed that they are universally accepted and taken for granted. The task then is not to develop a new type of Christian epistemology, but rather to explore new ways of articulating the dynamics of religious understanding so as to facilitate the appropriation of these traditional Christian concepts. The one thing needed therefore is not theoretical speculation about Christianity, but rather *edification:*

> There is one sure way of giving freshness and importance to the most *common-place* maxims—that of *reflecting* on them in direct reference to our own state and conduct, to our own past and

future being. . . . To restore a common-place truth to its first *un-common* lustre, you need only *translate* it into action. But to do this you must have reflected on its truth.[28]

Needless to say, much more can be said about Coleridge's approach to philosophy and religious reflection, especially with respect to the Kantian distinction he draws between understanding and reason, his views concerning the imagination, the role of the conscience, and the nature of faith.[29] My purpose has been simply to show that Coleridge's reflections on the nature of religious thinking provide an interesting and defensible alternative to the empiricist who insists that believers should be taken to task if they cannot defend their views by appealing to neutral epistemological considerations. This does *not* mean, of course, that the believer is somehow exempt from the obligation of giving reasons when reasons are called for. In an aphorism taken from the work of Henry More, Coleridge acknowledges that "Every one is *to give a reason of his faith.*"[30] The point, however, is that contrary to the Lockean picture of the ethics of belief, which requires people to defend their beliefs by appealing to objective reasons acceptable to any reasonable person, Coleridge grants the legitimacy of personal reasons, that is, reasons that already presuppose religious and spiritual concerns.

Of course, once we allow for personal reasons of this kind, it soon becomes clear why religious debate is often intractable. As we have seen, Locke's approach to the ethics of belief in the *Essay* is motivated by such a concern and an anxious desire to provide some type of epistemologically neutral framework to ensure the possibility for settling our disagreements. Although Locke himself suspects that some failures of reason are due to the fact that people allow other inclinations to override the inclination to pursue truth, he still hopes that a theory of human understanding will provide a reliable method for reaching some agreement and achieving knowledge.

Coleridge, on the other hand, rejects this kind of model of religious thinking and insists that it is a mistake to ignore the variety of ways an individual's personal interests and concerns inform their religious beliefs. Of course, if we accept Coleridge's approach and grant the importance that personal considerations have in the activity of giving reasons, we should not be surprised when people either do not understand each other or fail to acknowledge the relevance of each other's reasons. In short, there are limits to argument, and there is no reason to expect that the reasons I offer to defend my views on religion or morality will be acceptable to everyone. Such an impossible ideal is based on the Lockean dream of an epistemological utopia in which our conversation partners have been purged of all their particular and subjective interests. Locke's assumption is that it is precisely such particular and subjective interests that make truth-seeking impossible. His suspicion is that once we grant the legitimacy of personal reasons, it becomes difficult to see how inquiry can yield true knowledge. However, as writers such as Coleridge and Kierkegaard remind us, far from being an obstacle to religious knowledge, our acknowledgment of subjectivity is precisely what makes truth-seeking possible.

C. *Religious Belief and Personal Knowledge:*
   John Henry Newman

Unfortunately, however, Coleridge himself was not primarily a philosopher and as a result his insightful criticisms of empiricist epistemology tend to be impressionistic and underdeveloped. It is heartening to know then that these concerns are explored with more precision and rigor by the Victorian thinker John Henry Newman, who examines these issues in greater detail. In his well-known *Essay in Aid of a Grammar of Assent* (1870), for instance, Newman explores the relationship between human reasoning and religious belief and insists that an appeal to personal knowledge plays a legitimate and necessary role in the ethics of belief. Not surprisingly, he criticizes Locke's austere appeal to epistemic neutrality and concludes that such a standard of rationality is unrealistic and impractical. The problem, suggests Newman, is that Locke's deep-seated suspicion of religious enthusiasm leads him to criticize the natural role personal considerations play in the shaping of religious belief and to propose instead an unattainable ideal of human understanding. As Newman himself argues:

> Reasonings and convictions which I deem natural and legitimate, he apparently would call irrational, enthusiastic, perverse, and immoral; and that, as I think, because he consults his own ideal of how the mind ought to act, instead of interrogating human nature, as an existing thing, as it is found in the world.[31]

What then is Newman's alternative to Locke's overly rationalistic view of rationality? Newman's brief remark concerning Locke would seem to indicate that the ethics of belief should begin with an examination of how reasoning and argument actually work in the lives of ordinary people. In this respect, Newman anticipates the views of the later Wittgenstein who argues that the standards of what is to count as justification are not given a priori. If we want to understand the scope and limits of what is allowable with respect to the justification of religious claims, we must look rather to what counts as reason-giving in the context of a particular form of life.[32] It is simply a mistake to suppose, as Locke often does, that justification in moral and religious matters can be attained by an appeal to epistemologically neutral considerations. In most cases, a person's ability to recognize and acknowledge the force of an argument presupposes certain interests and concerns. What a person is willing to acknowledge with respect to such matters therefore depends on the many ways personal concerns inform reasoning and inference. In his discussion of Pascal's wager, for example, Newman rightly notes that the question of whether such argument can convince in a particular case turns on the individual's intellectual predisposition: "that standard will vary according to the respective dispositions, opinions, and experiences, of those to whom the argument is addressed. Thus, its value is a personal question. . . ."[33]

In his attempt to articulate in more detail a model of reasoning flexible enough to accommodate the wide variety of ways argument and justification sustain our beliefs, Newman appeals to what he call the "illative sense." Unfortunately, such an appeal to an illative *sense* easily lends itself to misunderstanding, especially in the context of the empiricist framework that underlies Newman's project. The temptation, of course, is to suppose that the illative sense is some kind of special psychological faculty that enables people to apprehend spiritual or moral truths. Nothing, however, could be further from the truth. In order to do justice to Newman's claims concerning the illative sense, we must remember that he is often constrained by the empiricist vocabulary, which he inherits from Locke and Hume, and that he often uses such terminology to undermine the very empiricist assumptions that underlie traditional epistemology.[34]

When Newman speaks of the illative sense he is not referring to some kind of special faculty but is simply trying to identify that aspect of human understanding that depends upon an individual's personal concerns:

> The aspect under which we view things is often intensely personal; nay, even awfully so, considering that, from the nature of the case, it does not bring home its idiosyncrasy either to ourselves or to others. Each of us looks at the world in his own way, and does not know that perhaps it is characteristically his own.[35]

At this point it might be worthwhile to point out that Newman's emphasis on the illative sense and the importance of personal knowledge has troubled many of his critics who suspect that appeals to such subjective considerations ultimately lead to an unacceptable form of fideism.[36] Such worries were especially troublesome to Newman's Victorian contemporaries whose naive empiricism made it difficult for them to make sense of Newman's insightful and innovative claims. Given the spirit of the age as well as Newman's clear and unequivocal language, such charges should not surprise us.

Throughout his writings, however, Newman makes it clear that there is no reason to suspect that a more flexible account of justification necessarily entails a pernicious form of subjectivism. He is quick to point out, for example, that although the force of an argument depends upon personal considerations, the truth of the matter is still objective. This is an important point to keep in mind since many people often mistakenly assume that any justification based on personal concerns necessarily leads to false or unjustified beliefs. The concern that appears to underlie the worries of these critics is similar to Locke's suspicion that an appeal to personal concerns opens the door to religious enthusiasm. According to such objections, the arbitrary nature of such concerns would seem to undermine the possibility of genuine knowledge. Once we grant legitimacy of what appears to be personal preference in the determination of our beliefs, it would seem that "anything goes."

Clearly, however, such criticisms are themselves suspect. For one thing, it is a mistake to suggest that any appeal to personal knowledge is merely an appeal to an individual's personal preference. One might argue, furthermore, that in some cases the ability to recognize and acknowledge the truth of the matter presupposes that the individual is personally engaged in the issue at hand. Such an assumption, I think, underlies the kind of claims made by Aristotle in his *Nicomachean Ethics* in which he insists that an education in ethics presupposes the presence of certain "subjective" interests and concerns: one cannot acquire an understanding of virtue unless one first *cares* about becoming a virtuous person. Aristotle himself, of course, insists that there is something which we might call "moral truth," but suggests that not everyone is equally disposed to recognize it. To a great extent, the ability to arrive at reasoned moral judgments and to discern the "moral truth" of the matter depends on whether a person has undergone the appropriate training and formation. On this kind of account, it is impossible to recognize the truth unless one already is in the process of developing a certain sort of character with the requisite virtues and emotions. In the world according to Aristotle, the recognition of truth depends on one's ability to see the world truly, which depends, in turn, on the kind of person one is.

Given this brief characterization of Aristotle's position, we should not be surprised to learn that Newman makes explicit mention of Aristotle in his discussion of the illative sense. In order to see why Newman's appeal to the illative sense is perfectly compatible with objectivity, it is important to pay special attention to the way he invokes Aristotle's notion of *phronesis* or "judgment" as the basis of his discussion. Like Aristotle, Newman believes that there is no logical decision procedure to ensure the truth of our judgments in moral matters. Any attempt to explicate Aristotle's moral epistemology would need to begin with the claim that a person's capacity for moral knowledge depends on his or her character. In a similar fashion Newman wants to suggest that the illative sense depends to a great extent on the character of the individual in question. Once again, such a claim does not amount to the denial that there is a truth of the matter. All it means is that the illative sense, or the ability to render reasoned judgments about the truth of religious matters, will depend on the shape of the individual's character in much the same way that *phronesis* or reasoned judgment in ethical matters depends on being a person of a certain sort. Newman makes this point explicitly in the following observation:

> Thus in concrete reasonings we are in great measure thrown back into that condition from which logic proposed to rescue us. We judge for ourselves, by our own lights, and on our own principles; and our criterion of truth is not so much the manipulation of propositions, as the intellectual and moral character of the person maintaining them, and the ultimate silent effect of his arguments or conclusions upon our minds.[37]

Needless to say there is much more that can be said about Newman's thought, particularly about his views on such issues as inference, assent, and the distinction between real and notional assents and certitude. Unfortunately, I cannot pretend to offer the kind of comprehensive account that would do justice to the breadth and scope of Newman's thought. My task has been more modest. What I have tried to show is that Newman's work provides important insights into the role of personal knowledge in the justification of religious beliefs. In particular, we have much to learn from Newman's appeal to the illative sense and his suggestion that our willingness to grant the force of an argument depends on a wide range of considerations such as our fundamental concerns, interests, and emotions. This does not mean, however, that "anything goes." The legitimacy of our beliefs does not depend on mere preference or arbitrary whim. Newman grants the necessity of epistemic constraints but agrees with Aristotle's suggestion that such constraints are primarily a function of the kind of people we are: justification in religious matters is radically self-involving. In the end, therefore, the ethics of belief is ultimately a question of character.

I want to claim then that Coleridge and Newman are right to emphasize the importance of personal knowledge. There is no way to escape the fact that the most important reasons we give to support our religious and moral convictions are *personal* reasons, in the sense that they are "self-involving." But if this is the case, we should not expect that the reasons we give will be acceptable to everyone. Once we grant the legitimacy of personal considerations and interests and acknowledge the essential role they play in shaping our reasons, it should come as no surprise that religious and moral debate *is* often intractable. There are limits to argument and sometimes these limits are simply a matter of our differences. Not surprisingly, this is a point that Newman recognizes when he considers the ways our characters limit what we can say and acknowledge in our disagreements with others. If personal knowledge is an ineliminable feature of this activity of reason-giving, it is no wonder why many arguments end without resolution:

> All reasoning from premises, and those premises arising (if it so happen) in their first elements from personal characteristics, in which men are in fact in essential and irremedial variance one with another, the ratiocinative talent can do no more than point out where the difference between them lies, how far it is immaterial, when it is worth while continuing an argument between them, and when not.[38]

The solution, however, is not to divest ourselves of these personal considerations or pretend that they have no bearing on our moral or religious convictions. Rather, we must acknowledge that at the limits of argument the ethics of belief is primarily a question of our willingness to clarify our commitments and to take responsibility for where we stand.

Notes

1. From "Self-Love," in *Literary Remains* (New York: Chelsea House, 1983), p. 125.

2. René Descartes, *Selected Philosophical Writings*, trans. John Cottingham, Robert Stoothoff, and Dugald Murdoch (Cambridge: Cambridge University Press, 1988), p. 22.

3. Ibid., p. 23

4. Ibid., p. 24.

5. Ibid.

6. Richard Popkin, *The History of Skepticism from Erasmus to Spinoza* (Berkeley: University of California Press, 1979).

7. Descartes, *Selected Writings*, p. 21.

8. See, for example, J. A. Passmore, "Locke and the Ethics of Belief," in *Rationalism, Empiricism, and Idealism*, ed. Anthony Kenny (Oxford: Clarendon Press, 1986), pp. 23–46. According to Passmore, Locke's extended critique of enthusiasm in later versions of the *Essay* is an attempt to explain why people are more likely to possess false beliefs rather than true ones. Locke's suggestion, claims Passmore, is that people "believe falsely, not as the result of inadequate evidence, but as a result of being dominated by powerful inclinations. . . . The rational man is then the man who is dominated by a passion for the truth, as distinct from party passions" (p. 46). I would like to note that my discussion of Locke is indebted to Passmore's insightful analysis of these issues.

9. John Locke, *An Essay Concerning Human Understanding*, ed. and intro. Peter H. Nidditch (Oxford: Clarendon Press, 1979), p. 697.

10. Ibid., p. 7.

11. Alasdair MacIntyre, *After Virtue*, 2d ed. (Notre Dame: University of Notre Dame Press, 1984).

12. It is worthwhile to note that not everyone shares MacIntyre's suggestion that concepts such as "rights" and "utility" are merely conceptual fictions intended to mask the erosion of our moral language. An alternative verdict on the development and value of moral philosophy since the Enlightenment has been provided by Jeffrey Stout who argues that the secularization of public discourse should be viewed as a response to growing tensions among competing religious groups. According to Stout, liberalism emerges not simply as an aberration of moral discourse, but rather as an attempt to create an epistemological space for public debate. As Stout himself insists, "It was partly because people recognized putting an end to religious warfare and intolerance as morally good—as rationally preferable to continued attempts at imposing a more nearly complete vision of the good by force—that liberal institutions have been able to get a foothold here and there around the globe." *Ethics after Babel: The Languages of Morals and Their Discontents* (Boston: Beacon Press, 1988), p. 212. Stout's continuing analysis of these issues has provided the inspiration for much of my discussion of Locke.

13. See Passmore, "Locke and the Ethics of Belief."

14. Locke, *Essay Concerning Human Understanding*, p. 715.

15. Ibid., pp. 530–31.

16. Ibid., p. 531.

17. Ibid., pp. 531–32.

18. Michael Polanyi, *Personal Knowledge* (Chicago: University of Chicago Press, 1962) has become something of a minor classic which has in turn influenced more recent attempts to rethink the important ways knowledge depends on our personal and subjective concerns.

19. John Henry Newman, *An Essay in Aid of a Grammar of Assent*, intro. Nicholas Lash (Notre Dame: University of Notre Dame Press, 1979), p. 300.

20. Although Coleridge's *Aids to Reflection* is not widely read among contemporary philosophers of religion, it is an important book that had a profound influence on many English-speaking thinkers of the nineteenth century including Horace Bushnell, Ralph Waldo Emerson, and John Henry Newman, to name just a few. In America the published book included an essay written by the Congregationalist James Marsh, whose discussion of Coleridge had a strong influence on the rise of Transcendentalism in New England. I hope my discussion will show that much can be gained from a serious reexamination of this work. For an informative discussion of Coleridge and Marsh see Bruce Kuklick, *Churchmen and Philosophers from Jonathan Edwards to John Dewey* (New Haven: Yale University Press, 1985), pp. 146–51.

21. Of the many helpful and insightful discussions of Coleridge's religious development, the best remains Basil Willey's classic study *Samuel Taylor Coleridge* (New York: W. W. Norton, 1973). For more detailed treatments of Coleridge's religious ideas see J. Robert Barth, S.J., *Coleridge and Christian Doctrine* (Cambridge: Harvard University Press, 1969), esp. chapter 2; and Claude Welch, "Samuel Taylor Coleridge" in *Nineteenth Century Religious Thought in the West*, vol. 2, ed. Ninian Smart, John Clayton, Steven T. Katz, and Patrick Sherry (Cambridge: Cambridge University Press, 1985), pp. 1–28.

22. J. Robert Barth, S.J., *Coleridge and Christian Doctrine*, pp. 1–13.

23. Samuel Taylor Coleridge, *Aids to Reflection* (New York: Chelsea House, 1983), p. xix.

24. Ibid., p. 134.

25. Ibid., p. 120.

26. Ibid., p. 272.

27. Ibid., p. 1.

28. Ibid.

29. For an excellent and thoughtful treatment of these issues see

Welch's article "Samuel Taylor Coleridge," in *Nineteenth Century Religious Thought*, pp. 1–28.

30. Coleridge, *Aids to Reflection*, p. 96.

31. Newman, *A Grammar of Assent*, p. 139.

32. There has been a revival of interest in Newman's thought among analytical philosophers which is connected to the growing realization that his work does foreshadow Wittgenstein's later philosophical views. J. M. Cameron, for example, has noted that much of what Newman has to say concerning doubt, belief, and justification anticipates some of the insights of Wittgenstein's *On Certainty* and that the tensions running through his work are due to the fact that the empiricist framework which he inherits from Locke and Hume tends to obscure his many important insights. Cameron's discussion of these issues can be found in his essay "John Henry Newman and the Tractarian Movement," in *Nineteenth Century Religious Thought in the West*, vol. 2, pp. 69–109. Perhaps the best discussion of the many ways Wittgensteinian concerns inform Newman's work is M. Jamie Ferreira's *Doubt and Religious Commitment: The Role of the Will in Newman's Thought* (Oxford: Clarendon Press, 1980), in which she appeals to the work of Wittgenstein and others, such as John Wisdom and Stephen Toulmin, to illuminate Newman's views on religious belief.

33. Newman, *A Grammar of Assent*, p. 245.

34. See J. M. Cameron, "John Henry Newman and the Tractarian Movement," esp. pp. 99ff.

35. Newman, *A Grammar of Assent*, p. 291.

36. These concerns have continued up until the present day. For the most recent characterization of Newman as a fideistic volitionalist, see Louis P. Pojman, *Religious Belief and the Will* (London: Routledge and Kegan Paul, 1986), esp. pp. 84–88.

37. Newman, *A Grammar of Assent*, p. 240.

38. Ibid., p. 283.

3

The Ethics of Belief
and the Meaning of Life

One need never have seen a Woody Allen film to appreciate the extent to which our concerns about love, death, and human suffering are tied to the more general question about the meaning of human existence. Although most of us do not generally ruminate about such matters and are likely to take such things for granted, at one time or another most of us will experience the wonder or perplexity that evokes both religious and philosophical questions about "the meaning of it all." As Arthur Schopenhauer reminds us, the human animal "marvels at its own works and asks itself what it itself is. And its wonder is the more serious, as here for the first time it stands consciously face to face with *death*, and besides the finiteness of all existence, the vanity and fruitlessness of all effort force themselves on it more or less."[1] Schopenhauer himself believes that such concerns support his thesis that human beings are basically "metaphysical animals" and that this need to ask metaphysical questions is the distinguishing characteristic of our species. And although we might wonder whether Schopenhauer overstates his case, he is right to highlight the way our need to ask metaphysical questions gives rise to both religious and philosophical speculation.

At this point though, we might still ask why a person's basic questions about the meaning of life should have anything to do with the ethics of belief. After all, few of us begin our lives by asking such deep and perplexing questions about cosmic issues such as God, death, and human suffering. On the contrary, if most religious believers view their lives in theistic terms, this is usually not because they have asked the "big questions," but rather because they have been nurtured in a particular religious community with specific beliefs and practices. According to this picture, our view of the world and ourselves is something we inherit as we are socialized into a particular group whose stories and rituals shape our self-interpretations. To use the language that has become fashionable among some philosophers and theologians, the meaning of our lives is a matter that has already been determined by the particular narrative that defines the scope and limits of what my community has to say concerning these questions. If we want to articulate in more detail such questions surrounding the meaning of life, we are invited to refine and sharpen those skills that might enable us to better understand the story. By learning to read sacred scriptures or by engaging in religious practice, believers gain a better appreciation of the way such fundamental questions about human life have been answered by the tradition.

There is, of course, some truth in this picture which situates questions about the meaning of life within specific traditions. By the same token, however, such an observation does not vitiate the basic point I wish to explore throughout the rest of this chapter; namely, that the ethics of religious belief is connected to a person's basic desire to see his life as a meaningful whole. The question is whether we can articulate what it means to satisfy this "metaphysical urge" and assess our various and competing solutions to the riddle of existence. We have already seen that it is a mistake to require a person to offer an impersonal justification for his or her religious beliefs for the simple fact that the reasons a person offers already presuppose religious concerns. But what exactly does this mean and why is it important? In this chapter I will answer these questions and argue that we should view a person's religious beliefs as constituting a life-view that enables people to make sense of their views about such concerns as death, suffering, and love. But since such "existential facts" are tied to a person's moods, emotions, and dispositions, it is impossible to discover some neutral description of these facts. To use the jargon of the philosophy of science, these "existential facts" are already "theory-laden" and thus reflect one's existential posture in the world.

What is particularly important with respect to our questions about the ethics of belief, however, is whether there is any way to assess such interpretations about the meaning of life. To what kind of criteria should we appeal? Does it make sense, for example, to suggest that we could *justify* a person's interpretation about the meaning of life? As I have already argued, since our life-views are already "theory-laden," it is difficult to specify precisely what neutral "justification" might mean in this context. But if we cannot speak of "justification," is it possible to at least speak of the "truth" of these interpretations? And if our interpretations about the meaning of life are not true in any straightforward sense, what might this mean with respect to the ethics of belief?

Throughout the rest of this chapter I would like to explore in more detail the nature of these concerns and argue that a person's religious beliefs are interpretations about life's meaning and that they differ from our other claims about the world insofar as they cannot be evaluated as true or false in any straightforward way. In order to present my case, I shall appeal to the work of Ludwig Wittgenstein who presents, I believe, the most insightful case for this kind of claim. It shall also become clear, I hope, that those who malign his position and characterize his views as a form of "fideism" are grossly mistaken. For when we examine Wittgenstein's later work in light of David Wiggins's writings on the meaning of life, the reasons for Wittgenstein's position become clear. In short, although a person's religious outlook can best be characterized as an attempt to make sense of life as a whole by providing a coherent account of the "existential data," such accounts are, to use Wiggins's language, "cognitively underdetermined." But to say that a set of beliefs is cognitively underdetermined is to say that they fall short of plain truth. In the end, such considerations should lead us to suspect that overly rationalistic approaches to the ethics of belief need to be critically appraised and replaced by a more holistic position.

A. Wittgenstein on Religious Belief

Influenced perhaps by Schopenhauer's claim that religion is a kind of "folk metaphysics"[2] and by Leo Tolstoy's literary explorations of such Schopenhauerian issues in novels such as *Anna Karenina*, Ludwig Wittgenstein maintains that religious beliefs involve basic judgments about the meaning of life. Although he articulates this basic claim in a variety of different ways throughout his life, his observations seem to suggest the following type of argument:

1. Religious beliefs are judgments about the meaning of life.
2. Judgments about the meaning of life fall short of plain truth.
3. Therefore, religious beliefs fall short of plain truth.

As it stands, this kind of argument can be interpreted in a wide variety of ways. Perhaps the most common but least defensible interpretation of this argument is the positivist one which is based on the controversial claim that religious beliefs, like metaphysical and moral beliefs, are meaningless and cannot therefore be assessed with respect to their truth or falsity. According to this interpretation, religious beliefs are at best expressions of a person's basic attitudes and emotions and as such have no cognitive significance. Among moral philosophers, this kind of thesis that reduces the meaning of moral and religious claims to expressions of a person's basic preferences has led some to defend a theory of moral and religious language more commonly known as emotivism.[3]

For better or worse, emotivism is a theory of moral language that has not fared well in recent years and the current orthodoxy is that this view is conceptually bankrupt. Since I accept the basic critique of emotivism offered by such thinkers as Alasdair MacIntyre,[4] among others, I will not belabor the point by rehearsing such arguments in detail. What I want to show is that even though we have good reasons to reject emotivism, there still might be an alternative way to interpret the argument presented above. The hope is that a more nuanced analysis of value statements might yield similar insights concerning the character of religious belief. So even though emotivism might prove to be a dead end, there might be alternatives open to support the general claim that religious beliefs involve practical judgments about the meaning of life and as such fall short of plain truth.

In order to see how this basic argument might lend itself to a number of different interpretations, it might be helpful to examine briefly Ludwig Wittgenstein's suggestive though enigmatic writings on the subject. In his early writings, such as the *Notebooks 1914–1916* and the *Tractatus Logico-Philosophicus*, Wittgenstein's views on religion and ethics are expressed in suggestive but rather opaque remarks concerning God and the meaning of life. The temptation of many more sober-minded philosophers is either to dismiss them as a symptom of this philosopher's youthful and thus excusable enthusiasm for Schopenhauer or simply to overlook them in order to get on with the more important if no less difficult task of explicating what the young Wittgenstein has to say about language and logic.[5] However, if we are to take seriously what Wittgenstein has to say regarding the *Tractatus* in an undated letter to his publisher, Ludwig von Ficker, there is good reason to take his enigmatic observations on the meaning of life much more seriously. As Wittgenstein himself insists: "I wanted to write that my work consists of two parts: the one which is here, and of everything which I have *not* written. And precisely this second part is the important one. For the Ethical is delimited from within, as it were, by my book; and I'm convinced that, *strictly* speaking, it can ONLY be delimited in this way."[6]

The point is that Wittgenstein's primary concern in his early writing is "ethical" and "religious," in the broad sense of these terms.[7] The difficult question, however, is whether it is possible to do justice to these "deep" problems without trivializing them. Wittgenstein expresses, for example, his own dissatisfaction with those who voice their concern with ethics and religion by "babbling" about it. In one sense then the motivation behind the brief enigmatic remarks on these subjects in his early work is therapeutic: to show us that the philosopher qua philosopher cannot help to answer the question of the meaning of life. The answer to this question rather has to do with the way one *leads* one's life.

In both the *Notebooks* and the *Tractatus* Wittgenstein does venture to pass beyond what can be said if only in the hope of pointing the way: to "show" us what it means to think about these strange sorts of questions. For example, with respect to the question of what it means to believe in God, Wittgenstein makes the following comments:

> To believe in God means to understand the question
> about the meaning of life.
> To believe in God means to see that the facts of the
> world are not the end of the matter.
> To believe in God means to see that life has a
> meaning.[8]

What is important to note is that like his intellectual mentors, Schopenhauer and Tolstoy, Wittgenstein begins with the assumption that religion is primarily a question of making sense out of one's life. Once again, at the risk of waxing existential, a person's belief in God cannot be understood independently of a person's need to view his life as a meaningful whole. Apparently this is the point behind Wittgenstein's remark that the person who believes in God sees that the "facts of the world are not the end of the matter." In the *Tractatus* this intuition is expressed in terms of the suggestion that even if all questions of fact could be answered, there would still be something important left over: "We feel that even when all *possible* scientific questions have been answered, the problems of life remain completely untouched. . . ."[9] The young Wittgenstein wants to call our attention to his intuition that a person's belief in God is not tied to matters of fact, that is, to questions of what is or is not the case. Belief in God, rather, is tied to a person's ability to find meaning in life, something that cannot be decided by an appeal to the facts. To put it another way: it is not the facts that give meaning to life but rather it is the way one leads one's life that makes the facts meaningful.[10]

Students of Wittgenstein have repeatedly noted that his initial difficulty in situating religious and moral beliefs stems in part from the problematic distinction between fact and value he is forced to draw on the basis of his so-called "picture-theory of meaning." According to this way of construing Wittgenstein's dilemma, the only propositions that possess a sense (*Sinn*) are those propositions that can picture a logically possible state of affairs. If this suggestion were right it surely would be difficult to see how values could be included as part of the furniture of the universe. If, for example, I were to say, "There is a portrait hanging on the wall," my words would possess a sense since they provide a picture of a possible state of affairs. If, however, I were to say, "The portrait is beautiful," I might feel at a loss if asked to specify in what way the statement could be said to mirror some possible state of affairs. It would seem that such a judgment cannot be a statement of fact because, according to Wittgenstein's early view, we simply cannot locate value, including answers to the question of life's meaning, in the world.

It is important to remember, though, that Wittgenstein's worries about value run deeper and need not be expressed solely as a way of dealing with certain problems generated by his picture-theory of meaning. Part of his concern is to show that questions of value, that is, questions concerning aesthetics, ethics, or religion, are not contingent in the same way facts are. They do not express what might or might not be the case but express rather necessary "truths" about life. As Wittgenstein himself insists in the *Tractatus*, "If there is any value that does have value, it must lie outside the whole sphere of what happens and is the case. For all that happens and is the case is accidental."[11] An expression of value therefore is not a statement about the facts because unlike the facts, value cannot be something accidental: like logic it must be a condition of the world. The problem, however, is that on Wittgenstein's terms it is impossible to admit that a noncontingent statement could possess a sense, so such a statement cannot even be regarded as a proposition. Not surprisingly then, Wittgenstein concludes that "it is impossible for there to be propositions of ethics."[12]

In his early work Wittgenstein presents a very mysterious picture of religious belief that is deceptively similar to a view that some characterize as Wittgensteinian Fideism.[13] When confronted by a religious believer and a person who sees no point in it, all we can say perhaps is that the world of the person who believes in God is different from the world of the person who does not believe in God. What is important to notice, moreover, is that in a work such as the *Tractatus*, the limits of what can be said with respect to religious questions are treated as problems that arise primarily because of a problematic distinction between fact and value. According to this line of thinking, religious questions are necessarily intractable and this has to do with the nature of language. Once we have a grasp of the essence of language, we will see why it is impossible for a person to *say* anything intelligible about the nature of logic, art, or the mystical. This is not to say, of course, that this feeling of the mystical is itself something suspicious or counterfeit. Religious believers need not abandon their beliefs about God. The point rather is that the young Wittgenstein seems to think that the only way to make sense of the peculiar nature of religious claims is to say that they show what cannot be said.

Of course, it was not long before Wittgenstein realized that the search for something like the "essence of language" is doomed to failure and that the philosopher should rest content with the more modest task of asking how language is actually used in human communities. The story of Wittgenstein's later views, however, is a complicated one and even the most seasoned Wittgenstein scholars sometimes find it difficult to agree about the shape of his philosophical development. For this reason I would like to focus not so much on the question of whether his later views concerning "language games" or "forms of life" can contribute anything in particular to our understanding of religious beliefs.[14] This, of course, has been the strategy of many of his later followers. Instead, I will take a different tack and focus on selected remarks about religion that provide a more fruitful approach to the question.

In his well-known "Lectures on Religious Belief,"[15] delivered by Wittgenstein in 1938, we find that although he expresses concerns similar to those in the earlier works, his approach is quite different. In particular, in these enigmatic but suggestive remarks Wittgenstein worries about the differences between people's beliefs on religious matters and wonders whether we can learn anything about religion by paying attention to these differences. What seems to trouble Wittgenstein is that it is often very difficult to articulate exactly what separates the believer from the unbeliever. What Wittgenstein is struggling to understand in these lectures is why such disagreements seem to run so deep.

In his opening remarks, for instance, Wittgenstein invites us to consider the case in which we want to understand someone's belief in the Last Judgment:

> Suppose that someone believed in the Last Judgement, and I don't, does this mean that I believe the opposite to him, just that there won't be such a thing? I would say: "not at all, or not always."[16]

Our first inclination, suggests Wittgenstein, might be to assume that the difference between the believer and the unbeliever stems simply from a disagreement over the facts: either there will be a Last Judgment or there will not—we will just have to wait and see. Wittgenstein quickly suggests, however, that it would be very misleading to characterize the disagreement in this way. In fact it is a mistake, continues Wittgenstein, to suppose that the believer and the unbeliever simply have contradictory beliefs about what is or is not the case: "If someone said: 'Wittgenstein, do you believe in this?' I'd say: 'No.' 'Do you contradict the man?' I'd say: 'No.' "[17]

The suggestion here that religious beliefs are neither true nor false is much in keeping with the views that Wittgenstein sets forth in the

Notebooks and the *Tractatus* in which he insists that religious belief is not a matter of fact. It is important to note, however, that he no longer supports this contention by appealing to the distinction between facts and value as he did in the earlier work. So even though Wittgenstein still wants to insist that disagreements about religion are not disagreements about the facts, he does not base this claim on what he later admits to be mistaken views concerning the essence of language. The point, rather, which is made more explicit in the *Philosophical Investigations*, is that if there are such disagreements, it is *not* because of problems raised by a troublesome distinction between fact and value. The basis of the type of disagreements that interest Wittgenstein in his later work is to be found in what he refers to as the different "pictures" that give shape and meaning to a person's life:

> Suppose someone is ill and he says: "This is a punishment," and I say: "If I am ill, I don't think of punishment at all." If you say: "Do you believe the opposite?"—you can call it believing the opposite, but it is entirely different from what we would normally call believing the opposite. I think differently, in a different way. I say different things to myself. I have different pictures.[18]

Wittgenstein's remark that the believer and the unbeliever have different "pictures" which determine how each regards punishment seems to express a view similar to William James's observation that the spiritual attitude involves the longing to read the facts religiously. Like James, Wittgenstein wants to call our attention to the way religious beliefs can be understood as an expression of a person's orientation to life as a whole. In this respect, both would want to claim, I think, that it is a mistake to construe religious beliefs as special kinds of knowledge claims about the world. Unlike knowledge claims, which can be expressed in straightforward propositions concerning what is or is not the case, religious beliefs are an expression of what James calls a certain way of reading or interpreting the facts. In the *Tractatus* Wittgenstein attempts to express this kind of intuition about religious belief when he speaks of what it means to view the world as a limited whole. And although he later abandons this way of speaking, he makes a similar point when he draws the analogy between religious beliefs and "pictures" that enable a person to order experience in this way. Even as late as 1947 we find that Wittgenstein continues to characterize religious belief in these terms:

> It strikes me that a religious belief could only be something like a passionate commitment to a system of reference. Hence, although it's *belief*, it's really a way of living, or a way of assessing

life. It's passionately seizing hold of this interpretation. Instruction in a religious faith, therefore, would have to take the form of a portrayal, a description of that system of reference, while at the same time being an appeal to conscience.[19]

Wittgenstein's appeal to a "system of reference" admittedly sounds a bit flat-footed when taken out of context. The point he wishes to make, however, is a subtle one and runs through all of his writings on the subject. Very simply, Wittgenstein, like William James, wants to remind us that when we reflect on religious belief, we must be wary of treating it as just another kind of knowledge claim that can be reduced to a set of propositions about "the facts." And yet, he would also reject his own earlier view that consigns religious beliefs to a completely separate realm of value. The question is whether there is a third alternative that enables us to account for the strange character of religious disagreements and still steer clear of the troublesome fact-value distinction.

If, as Wittgenstein insists, religious beliefs are tied in an important way to a person's basic cares and concerns, they might be better viewed as an interpretation that enables a person to make sense of life as a whole. That is to say, they do not provide us with new facts, but rather a new way of organizing the facts. Moreover, Wittgenstein seems to agree with thinkers such as Søren Kierkegaard and William James, both of whom agree that the way we organize "the facts" depends on our moods, emotions, and dispositions. One's ability to acknowledge the "point" behind a person's religious convictions then demands much more than an analysis to determine whether holding such beliefs is rational or epistemically permissible in some minimal sense. Perhaps the greatest lesson we can learn from Wittgenstein is his suggestion that we understand a person's religious beliefs when we see the connection between this longing to read the facts religiously and the shape of the person's life as a whole:

> If someone who believes in God looks round and asks "Where does everything I see come from?", "Where does all this come from?", he is *not* craving for a (causal) explanation; and his question gets its point from being the expression of a certain craving. He is, namely, expressing an attitude toward all explanations.—But how is this manifested in his life?[20]

In the end there is something important behind our reformulation of the Wittgensteinian maxim: the world of the person who believes in God is different from the world of the person who does not believe in God. However, our sense that it is difficult to articulate the basis of this kind of disagreement is not due to an overdrawn and unacceptable distinction between fact and value. The difference between the two people has more to do with the different "pictures" or interpretations that give shape and meaning to their experience. It is important to stress, however, that there is no reason why one person could not understand another's picture, nor is there any reason to rule out the possibility of discussion. Wittgenstein's "private language argument" should serve as a warning against the ever-present temptation to view our "pictures" as "private affairs." As Wittgenstein himself confesses, however, it is one thing to understand a person's "picture" of life and quite another thing to endorse it as one's own.

From this brief survey of Wittgenstein's thought it should be clear that although he never abandons his basic view that religious beliefs are judgments about the meaning of life, his later views hardly warrant the charge of fideism. However, when he stops worrying about the distinction between fact and value suggested in his early work, he runs into difficulties when he tries to articulate an alternative that might account for the peculiar nature of the believer's attempt to make sense of his life. The specific problem, as he suggests, is that one's religious beliefs elude our attempts to assess them as either true or false in a straightforward way. Clearly, his appeals to notions such as "pictures" or "systems of reference" can be viewed as suggestive attempts to solve this particular problem. And although his observations are not always presented in a rigorous and systematic fashion, the intuitions that guide his investigations are, I believe, basically correct. The question then is whether there is another way to explicate and clarify his insights.

B.   *David Wiggins on the Meaning of Life*

In order to appreciate the significance of Wittgenstein's position on these matters I would like to appeal to the work of David Wiggins, whose essay "Truth, Invention, and the Meaning of Life"[21] can be invoked to defend Wittgenstein's later insights on the nature of religious belief. At first glance such a claim may sound strange, given the fact that this article begins as a critique of naive noncognitivism and raises the question of whether considerations of truth should figure into our reflections on life's meaning. By the end of the article, however, it becomes clear that Wiggins believes there is a grain of truth in noncognitivism—at least with respect to our judgments about the meaning of life—and that an appeal to what he calls the "doctrine of cognitive underdetermination" can perhaps grant us the insights of noncognitivism without the liabilities. We can, I believe, appeal to Wiggins's discussion of these issues to show that in a similar fashion there is an important grain of truth to be found in Wittgenstein's later views on religion.

As the discussion unfolds, it becomes increasingly clear that Wiggins's primary targets are writers such as Jean-Paul Sartre, R. M. Hare, and Richard Taylor, all of whom propose an extreme and unacceptable form of noncognitivism by arguing that value and meaning in life are simply the creation of the human will. Following the lead of Albert Camus, for example, Richard Taylor invokes the myth of Sisyphus as the classic example of our human-all-too-human struggle to find meaning in life. He notes that any attempt to view our lives from a distance, "the view from nowhere," to borrow a phrase from Thomas Nagel, seems to highlight the pointlessness of many of our activities. On the face of it, suggests Taylor, it is difficult to imagine any intrinsic value in life to vindicate our hope that it might be inherently meaningful. Like Schopenhauer, clearly the source of his inspiration in these matters, Taylor seems to think that the activities that comprise a human life are, on their own terms, pointless and arbitrary. Given this bleak and rather pessimistic picture, Taylor concludes that if our lives are meaningful, it is only by virtue of fundamental *choice* to invest them with meaning. For even though the point of life "is simply to be living," we must remember, concludes Taylor, that "the meaning of life is from within us, it is not bestowed from without."[22]

Although Wiggins identifies people such as Taylor as his primary targets, it is clear that his critique of naive noncognitivism would be equally applicable to Wittgenstein's early views on ethics and religion, especially with respect to the views proposed in the *Notebooks* and the *Tractatus*. Like Taylor, whose view seems to presuppose a radical distinction between fact and value, Wittgenstein begins his career with the claim that religious value cannot be found in the world. Not suprisingly then Wittgenstein's early writing on ethics and religion also anticipate Taylor's "volitionalism" when, for example, he suggests that what is required is some kind of leap of faith that might result in a radically different perspective on the world. For this reason, we should not be surprised that Wittgenstein encourages himself to "live happy," [23] a piece of existential advice he records in his *Notebooks*.

Needless to say, Wiggins would probably be suspicious of Wittgenstein's early position, to the extent that it tends to resemble the Taylor-Schopenhauer account of which he is so critical. Aside from the fact that such an account is contrary to our phenomenological intuition—namely, that we cannot *choose* to make a meaningless life meaningful by arbitrary fiat—there are other problems. For example, there is something to be said with respect to whether the meaningfulness of a life might depend on "how well or badly our strivings are apt to turn out."[24] In addition, the noncognitivist cannot do justice to our sense that there might be relevant differences that distinguish competing solutions to the dilemma of existence: although there does not appear to a be a single and simple "truth" of the matter, it is possible to compare and assess differing answers to the question. Such considerations lead Wiggins to ask whether the naive noncognitivist gives up too much and whether there is a better way of viewing the problem.

As already mentioned, what makes Wiggins's essay relevant for our present purposes is not only his sharp critique of naive noncognitivism, but his suggestion that noncognitivism might still include an important insight. More specifically, Wiggins seems to share Wittgenstein's belief that our judgments about the meaning of life fall short of plain truth. Of particular importance in this regard is Wiggins's observation that although we expect all our true beliefs about the world to be reconcilable, since this is one of the marks of plain truth,[25] this is something we have no reason to expect with respect to judgments about life's meaning. According to Wiggins, even if it should happen to turn out that everyone were to agree about such "existential" judgments, we still would not be entitled to conclude that such judgments are a matter of plain truth since convergence is not simply a matter of intersubjective agreement.[26] In order to determine whether a claim qualifies as a candidate for plain truth, it is not enough to point out that all of our judgments about the claim might converge. Plain truth also requires that the *best* explanation for *why* they converge is the way the world really is. Since, argues Wiggins, there is no way to defend the suggestion that our judgments about the meaning of life meet this requirement, we are entitled to conclude that they fall short of plain truth.

What then is Wiggins's final verdict and what significance does it have for our understanding of religious beliefs? Although we have good reason to reject the more flat-footed varieties of noncognitivism, its "distinctive nucleus," what Wiggins calls the doctrine of cognitive underdetermination, can allow us to grant the insights of noncognitivism without becoming noncognitivists. Wiggins summarizes this view in the following terms:

> What the new position will say is that, in so far as anything matters, and in so far as human life has the meaning we think it has, that possibility is rooted in something that is arbitrary, contingent, unreasoned, objectively non-defensible—and not one whit the less arbitrary, contingent and indefensible by virtue of the fact that the unconstrained inventive processes underlying it have been gradual, unconscious, and communal. Our form of life—or that in our form of life which gives individual lives meaning—is not something that men have ever (as they are apt to say) found or discovered. It is not something that they can

criticize or regulate or adjust with an eye to what is true or correct or reasonable.[27]

At this point I want to stress that although Wiggins's critique of noncognitivism would rule out the plausibility of the kind of position we find in the *Tractatus*, his more constructive remarks would support Wittgenstein's later views on religion, which clearly suggest the cognitive underdetermination of religious belief. As we have seen, throughout his life Wittgenstein characterizes religious beliefs as judgments about the meaning of life. After abandoning his earlier views on language he is forced to find another way of articulating this view and opts for metaphors such as "pictures" or "systems of reference" in order to characterize his holistic view of religious belief. Denying that we should characterize a person's religious beliefs either as the creation of an arbitrary will or as a reflection of the "plain truth," Wittgenstein searches throughout his later writings for some way to escape this dilemma and seems to advance a position similar to the one defended by Wiggins who concludes:

> In living a life there is no truth, and there is nothing *like* regular truth, for us to aim at. Anybody who supposes that the assertibility of 'I must do this' or the assertibility of 'This is the way for me to live, not that' consists in their plain truth is simply deluded.[28]

In conclusion, I believe we should follow the lead of Wiggins and appeal to the cognitive underdetermination of religious beliefs as a plausible and defensible reconstruction of Wittgenstein's later views concerning ethics and religion. Not only does such an approach make the best sense out of Wittgenstein, it also illuminates several important issues of concern to theologians and philosophers of religion. First of all, this position does not entail any form of volitionalism, which is another way of saying that we need not invoke the will to explain the acquisition of religious belief. Because a meaningful life can never be created by an arbitrary act of will, there is no reason to worry that a person's religious beliefs might be based on some form of blind commitment or leap of faith.

Second, the doctrine of cognitive underdetermination allows for an axiological pluralism. This means that there is no reason to expect that there should be one single answer to questions about the meaning of life. As Wittgenstein rightly notes throughout his work, people frame their basic concerns and commitments by appealing to different "pictures." In some cases, a person's attempt to view his or her life as a meaningful whole will involve religious claims. However, if Wiggins is right, there is no reason to expect that everyone will see or acknowledge the point behind a person's religious beliefs. Because claims concerning the meaning of life fall short of plain truth, there is no reason to expect that believers and nonbelievers will ultimately reach agreement on these important matters.

The doctrine of cognitive underdetermination has a third and particularly relevant implication for theologians and philosophers which stems from Wiggins's suggestion that reflection concerning the meaning of life needs to take more seriously the complexity of what it means to live a life. The problem, says Wiggins, is that ethicists have traditionally tended to offer theoretical accounts of morality in terms of general and elusive notions such as rights or utility, and that this approach has blinded them to the rich and nuanced texture of our moral lives. For this reason, Wiggins suggests that the moral theorist has much to learn from literature, which invites us to explore the question of life's meaning by attending to our world in all its existential detail. Like Iris Murdoch and Martha Nussbaum,[29] both of whom insist that literature provides a vital resource for moral reflection, Wiggins believes that much can be gained if we pay more attention to the way basic issues about the meaning of human life are explored in literature. This does not mean, of course, that we should collapse the distinction between literature and philosophy, as many more radical proposals suggest. Rather, the moral theorist and, I would add, the philosopher of religion, should view the suggestion as an invitation to broaden and enrich our understanding of what it means to engage in moral and religious reflection. As Wiggins suggests:

> Working within an intuitionism or moral phenomenology as tolerant of low-grade non-behavioural evidence as is literature (but more obsessively elaborative of the commonplace, and more theoretical, in the interpretive sense, than literature), he has to appreciate and describe the quotidian complexity of what is experientially involved in a man's seeing a point in living.[30]

Such considerations seem to be much in keeping with the concerns of those moral philosophers and theologians who maintain that there is much to be gained from a renewed appreciation of the way narratives frame our basic perspectives and ultimate valuations about life's meaning. Among moral thinkers such as Alasdair MacIntyre and followers of the theologian Hans Frei, whose *The Eclipse of Biblical Narrative*[31] has set the agenda of many theologians for more than a decade, appeals to narrative have provided liberating and fruitful insights. The question that is often raised with respect to such appeals, however, is whether narratives can in fact be assessed with respect to their plain truth. Some thinkers[32] seem to believe that there is no reason why appeals to narrative should exclude any consideration of truth. However, if the account I have outlined is correct, then such claims made for narrative should be much more modest. For if the value of narrative is its capacity to frame and shape our basic perspectives about life's meaning, and if such interpretations fall short of plain truth, then we must give up the hope that there is something like "narrative truth," at least in the literal sense of the term. Those thinkers, such as Garrett Green and Stephen Crites, who suggest at times that there is something to this notion, base their case, I think, on a misleading equivocation of the terms "truth" and "truthfulness." Unfortunately, if religious beliefs are cognitively underdetermined in the way I think Wittgenstein suggests, then it might be more helpful to refine our claims for narrative by making this distinction more explicit and by acknowledging that when it comes to narrative, perhaps truthfulness is all we can hope for.

Finally, I would like to suggest that these claims regarding the cognitive underdetermination of religious beliefs can also make sense of the variety of ways a person can find or lose faith. The traditional tendency to treat one's religious beliefs as atomistic claims isolated from one's concerns about the meaning of one's life ignores the extent to which changes in a person's religious outlook tend to be "unreasoned." To use a Wittgensteinian turn of phrase, a person's religious life waxes and wanes as a whole and for this reason it is impossible to articulate the reasons for the discovery or loss of faith independently of these larger concerns. For this reason, I prefer to speak not of the corrigibility of a person's religious beliefs, but rather of their fragility, a theme I will explore in more detail in a later chapter. What I want to emphasize at this point is that the cognitive underdetermination of religious beliefs raises a wide variety of interesting and fruitful questions and would seem to support a more holistic approach to the ethics of belief.

Notes

1. Arthur Schopenhauer, *The World as Will and Representation*, vol. 2, trans. E. F. J. Payne (New York: Dover Books, 1966), p. 160.

2. Schopenhauer develops this interesting and provocative thesis in his dialogue "On Religion" in *Parerga and Paralipomena*, vol. 2, trans. E. F. J. Payne (Oxford: Clarendon Press, 1974), pp. 324–94.

3. The classic examples of this theory are defended by A. J. Ayer, *Language, Truth and Logic* (New York: Dover Publications, 1952) and C. L. Stevenson, *Ethics and Language* (New Haven: Yale University Press, 1945).

4. Alasdair MacIntyre, *After Virtue*, 2d ed. (Notre Dame: University of Notre Dame Press, 1984), pp. 6–35.

5. For a recent treatment that takes seriously the influence of Schopenhauer on Wittgenstein's early writings, see Richard R. Brockhaus, *Pulling up the Ladder: The Metaphysical Roots of Wittgenstein's "Tractatus Logico-Philosophicus"* (La Salle: Open Court, 1990).

6. *Wittgenstein: Sources and Perspectives*, ed. C. G. Luckhardt (Sussex: Harvester Press, 1979), pp. 94–95.

7. For an insightful biographical treatment of Wittgenstein's early reflections on these issues see Ray Monk, *Ludwig Wittgenstein: The Duty of Genius* (New York: The Free Press, 1990), esp. pp. 137–66.

8. Ludwig Wittgenstein, *Notebooks 1914–1916*, 2d ed., trans. G. E. M. Anscombe (Chicago: University of Chicago Press, 1979), p. 74e.

9. Ludwig Wittgenstein, *Tractatus Logico-Philosophicus*, trans. D. F. Pears and B. F. McGuinness (London: Routledge and Kegan Paul, 1972), 6.52.

10. Something similar to the Euthyphro question seems to run through many of Wittgenstein's dark sayings on the meaning of life. I have noted this point in connection with what Kierkegaard has to say regarding similar issues in "Kierkegaard and Euthyphro," *Philosophy* (April 1987): pp. 221–26.

11. Wittgenstein, *Tractatus Logico-Philosophicus*, 6.41.

12. Ibid., 6.42.

13. See, for example, Kai Nielsen, *An Introduction to the Philosophy of Religion* (New York: St. Martin's Press, 1982), esp. chapters 4 and 5. Although Nielsen's book claims to be an introduction to the philosophy of religion, his concerns are more specific. Most of the book is devoted to a critical examination of the way Wittgenstein's thought has been appropriated by some philosophers of religion. Nielsen is the thinker originally responsible for coining the phrase "Wittgensteinian Fideism" as a term of derision.

14. A complete and detailed discussion of what has become a "subfield" of Wittgensteinian scholarship is beyond the scope of this essay. But perhaps the most well-known appropriation of these notions can be found in the work of D. Z. Phillips, especially his *The Concept of Prayer* (New York: Seabury Press, 1981) and his collection of essays *Faith and Philosophical Enquiry* (London: Routledge and Kegan Paul, 1970). Phillips's work itself has generated much discussion and heated debate and

his well-known article "Religious Beliefs and Language Games" in the second collection listed above proposes what might be called the classical version of Wittgensteinian Fideism. Phillips has answered the charges of critics such as Nielsen in his book *Belief, Change & Forms of Life* (Atlantic Highlands: Humanities Press, 1986). A thoughtful and interesting response to this approach is Patrick Sherry's *Religion, Truth, and Language-Games* (New York: Barnes and Noble, 1977).

15. Ludwig Wittgenstein, *Lectures and Conversations on Aesthetics, Psychology, and Religious Belief*, ed. Cyril Barrett (Berkeley: University of California Press, 1968), pp. 53–72.

16. Ibid., p. 53.

17. Ibid.

18. Ibid., p. 55.

19. Ludwig Wittgenstein, *Culture and Value*, ed G. H. von Wright, trans. Peter Winch (Chicago: University of Chicago Press, 1977), p. 64e.

20. Ibid., p. 85e.

21. David Wiggins, "Truth, Invention, and the Meaning of Life," in *Needs, Values, Truth* (Oxford: Basil Blackwell, 1987), pp. 87–137.

22. Taylor's views concerning the value of life are developed in the final chapter of his book "The Meaning of Life" in *Good and Evil: A New Direction* (London: Macmillan Company), pp. 256–68.

23. Wittgenstein, *Notebooks 1914–1916*, p. 75e.

24. Wiggins, "Truth, Invention, and the Meaning of Life," p. 98.

25. Ibid., p. 115. In this particular article Wiggins summarizes what he takes to be the five marks of plain truth. A more detailed presentation of these criteria can be found in his article "Truth as Predicated of Moral Judgments," in the volume *Needs, Values, Truth* where he gives the following list on pages 147–48.
 (1) Truth is a primary dimension of assessment for beliefs and for sentences that can express or report beliefs;
 (2) If x is true, then x will under favorable circumstances command convergence, and the best explanation of the existence of this convergence will require the actual truth of x;
 (3) For any x, if x is true then x has content; and if x has content then x's truth cannot simply consist in x's being itself a belief, or in x's being something believed or willed or . . .

(4) Every true belief (every truth) is true in virtue of something;
(5) If x_1 is true and x_2 is true, then their conjunction is true.

26. Ibid., pp. 149–51.

27. Wiggins, "Truth, Invention, and the Meaning of Life," p. 124.

28. Ibid., p. 126.

29. The complex relationship between moral reflection and literature has been the continuing focus of Nussbaum's writings, in particular
her well-known but controversial study, *The Fragility of Goodness: Luck
and Ethics in Greek Tragedy and Philosophy* (Cambridge: Cambridge
University Press, 1986). She continues her ongoing discussion of ethics
and literature in her recent collection of essays, *Love's Knowledge: Essays on Philosophy and Literature* (New York: Oxford University Press,
1990).

30. Wiggins, "Truth, Invention, and the Meaning of Life," p. 137.

31. Hans W. Frei, *The Eclipse of Biblical Narrative: A Study in
Eighteenth and Nineteenth Century Hermeneutics* (New Haven: Yale
University Press, 1975). The influence of Frei's work can be seen in the recent collection of essays *Scriptural Authority and Narrative Interpretation*, ed. Garrett Green (Philadelphia: Fortress Press, 1987).

32. See, for example, Garrett Green, "'The Bible As . . .': Fictional
Narrative and Scriptural Truth," in *Scriptural Authority and Narrative
Interpretation*, pp. 79–96, as well as Stephen Crites, "The Spatial Di-
mensions of Narrative Truthtelling," in the same volume, pp. 97–118.

4

Religious Belief and Self-Understanding

In the previous three chapters I have argued that, although the assessment of a person's religious convictions is an issue involving the ethics of belief, it is a mistake to assume that this should be viewed primarily as an epistemological concern, in the narrow sense of the term. Thinkers as diverse as Coleridge, Kierkegaard, and Wittgenstein have each in his own way insisted that religious beliefs do not lend themselves to this type of analysis and conclude instead that they should be viewed as answers to a person's most basic and fundamental questions about the meaning of life. In this chapter I would like to continue this Wittgensteinian mode of inquiry by considering in more detail how one's religious beliefs are tied to the attempt to make sense out of one's life. For if Wittgenstein is right, it is a mistake to assess a person's religious convictions in an objective fashion as beliefs about what is or is not the case. Inspired by Kierkegaard, Wittgenstein asks us to consider the problem as a "subjective" one and suggests that a person's religious beliefs can best be understood in terms of an attempt to arrive at some type of self-understanding about what makes life meaningful.

The issue seems to be that unlike some beliefs, such as my belief that it is cold in Denmark today, religious beliefs, such as the belief in God's existence, are tied in a special way to a person's sense of self. Although there is always some danger in waxing poetic, religious beliefs possess an existential aspect, which is another way of saying that they are intimately connected to those commitments, projects, and purposes that give shape and meaning to a person's life. For this reason, an analysis such as John Locke's, which is limited to a consideration of whether it is epistemically permissible to believe certain propositions, fails to do justice to the complex ways these beliefs may be tied to our self-constitutive concerns and commitments. So once one expands one's analysis to include the assessment not only of one's beliefs, but also of one's desires, purposes, and concerns, a whole host of new and interesting questions emerges.

For example, if the criteria for assessing our life-views about life's meaning are not simply epistemic ones, what are they? If we follow the lead of Martha Nussbaum and Stanley Cavell, among others, the most fruitful place to begin is literature: plays, movies, and novels. One might even go so far as to say that the criteria for assessing and evaluating our judgments about life's meaning have more in common with aesthetic criteria than they do with epistemic criteria.[1] Therefore, if we want to understand how interpretations about life's meaning emerge and develop over the course of a person's life, it would be most helpful to begin with a novel that treats such issues. Leo Tolstoy's masterpiece *Anna Karenina* provides an excellent opportunity for this kind of exploration.

Before I turn to consider Tolstoy's response to these issues, I should note that once the ethics of belief becomes a question of a certain type of critical self-reflection, new problems and difficulties emerge. For one thing, although religious beliefs are tied to the believer's attempt to make sense of his or her life and to come to a certain kind of self-understanding, there is no guarantee that this type of reflection will always sustain that person's beliefs. In fact, the type of subjective reflection that I wish to defend in this chapter renders such beliefs vulnerable in a wide variety of ways. For instance, although a person's religious convictions may have once enabled him or her to make the most sense of life as a whole, he or she may have changed in such a way as to render these former commitments unintelligible. The problem is compounded by the fact that we are always in a position to entertain a wide variety of competing ways of making sense of our lives and that there is no way to ensure that conflicting commitments and loyalties may not lead to the erosion of our religious beliefs.

Another question we need to explore in more detail is whether there are limits to the type of critical self-reflection that I take to be the center of the ethics of belief. On the one hand, it would seem that such self-reflection provides an important means for guarding against the danger of self-deception. It is widely known that there are many ways a person can refuse to acknowledge that certain commitments and loyalties that once provided an existential "center of gravity" no longer give meaning and shape to his or her life. For this reason, what is required is what Wittgenstein once termed "a certain suspicion of oneself." On the other hand, I want to show that it is equally clear why a radical questioning of all one's basic concerns and commitments is disastrous. Such a radical skepticism would only succeed in rendering most of one's life meaningless. For this reason, there is no denying that there are limits to the "will-to-truth" and that the type of approach sometimes advocated by thinkers such as Friedrich Nietzsche in his more radical moments is pernicious to the extent that it threatens to undermine in an unacceptable way the stability of one's life as a whole. So although the ethics of belief is primarily a question of critical self-reflection, it is important to maintain a balance in order to avoid both the vice of self-deception as well as the vice of rootless skepticism.

A. *Finding Meaning in Life: Tolstoy's* Anna Karenina

> Give me a lover, he will feel that of which I speak: give me one who longs, who hungers, who is a thirsty pilgrim in this wilderness, sighing for the springs of his eternal homeland: give me such a man, he will know what I mean.
>
> *St. Augustine*[2]

The attempt to make sense of one's life begins with a sense of perplexity, a sense that existence is a deep riddle that cries out for a solution. If, for example, we consider the story of Konstantin Levin, one of the central characters in Leo Tolstoy's *Anna Karenina*,[3] we discover the extent to which a genuine concern for this kind of question can shape a person's entire life. Although we are constantly reminded that Levin shows little interest or sympathy for organized religion or the doctrines of traditional Christianity, he is clearly obsessed with those religious concerns expressed by limit questions about the meaning of life. Early in the novel, we learn that Levin, owner of a large country estate, is desperately in love with Kitty Shtcherbatskaya, who initially refuses Levin's marriage proposal in the hope of receiving an offer from Count Vronsky. As it turns out Vronsky never proposes to Kitty but becomes involved with Anna Karenina in the famous ill-fated love affair that is the center of dramatic interest throughout the novel.

After Kitty's initial refusal to marry him, Levin returns to his estate at Pokrovskoe in the hope that a return to a simpler life will help him to discover something that might make his life meaningful. Under a starlit country sky, he acknowledges that his task is to make some sense out of his life and begins by entertaining the possibility of solving the riddle by "the renunciation of his old life, of his utterly useless education."[4] His hope is that the purity and simplicity of country living might be the solution to his dilemma. He even begins to imagine what his life would look like if he were to abandon his present way of life to marry a peasant woman. In the midst of his reverie, however, Levin is shocked when he catches a glimpse of Kitty riding in a nearby coach. Suddenly, he realizes that the possibility of such a simple life, which seemed to be the answer just a moment earlier, would merely be an escape from what he really cared about most. In the end he acknowledges that any attempt to make sense out of his life must take account of his deep love for Kitty:

> He could not be mistaken. There were no other eyes like those in the world. There was only one creature in the world that could concentrate for him all the brightness and meaning of life. It was she. It was Kitty. . . . And everything that had been stirring Levin during that sleepless night, all the resolutions he had made, all vanished at once. He recalled with horror his dreams of marrying a peasant girl. There only, in the carriage that had crossed over to the other side of the road, and was rapidly disappearing, there only could he find the solution of the riddle of his life, which had weighed so agonizingly upon him as of late.[5]

If the answer to the riddle of life were this easy, we would expect that his marriage to Kitty might put an end to his perplexity. It is clear, however, that Levin's concerns run much deeper and that his desire to make sense out of his life is motivated by what appear to be more fundamental and religious concerns. Even as Levin recites his vows during the wedding ceremony, he has a vague apprehension that his life is still not intelligible to him: "Levin felt more and more that all his ideas of marriage, all his dreams of how he would order his life, were mere childishness, and that it was something he had not understood hitherto, and now understood less than ever, though it was being performed upon him."[6] Far from making his life more intelligible his marriage to Kitty turns out to make the riddle of the meaning of life more mysterious and enigmatic than ever.

As we explore the source of Levin's preoccupations with these kinds of issues, we discover that he is especially perplexed by those events in his life that challenge his understanding of what is important in human life. The two central events in the novel that lead Levin to ask what we have characterized as limit questions are the death of his brother Nikolay and the birth of his son. The problem is that these kinds of limit situations, to borrow a phrase from Karl Jaspers, are disturbing to Levin precisely because they disturb the stability of his life. So when, for example, Levin confronts his consumptive brother, he is challenged to acknowledge how vulnerable and fragile our lives can be. His initial response, however, is not a loving acceptance of our fragility, but rather an insistence that life must be affirmed *in spite* of death:

> Levin said what he had genuinely been thinking of late. He saw nothing but death or the advance towards death in everything. . . . Life had to be got through somehow till death did come. Dark-

ness had fallen upon everything for him; but just because of this darkness he felt that the one guiding clue in the darkness was his work, and he clutched it and clung to it with all his strength.[7]

Nikolay's illness serves to remind Levin of the wisdom found in the book of Ecclesiastes, and it is interesting to note that he not only seems to acknowledge the truth of the claim "Vanity of vanities, all is vanity" but also takes seriously the preacher's recommendation that one should seek solace in one's labor: "There is nothing better for a man that he should eat and drink, and find enjoyment in his toil . . ."(Eccles. 2:24).

Levin eventually discovers, however, that the riddle posed by the inevitability of death cannot be solved by hiding behind the fragile facade of one's everyday concerns. A loyal devotion to one's vocation might provide temporary comfort to some, but one can hardly expect that a dedication to one's work can give meaning to a life when the possibility of death lurks around the corner. Levin himself is finally forced to come to terms with the reality of death when Nikolay returns to the country later in the story: "The sight of his brother, and the nearness of death, revived in Levin that sense of horror in the face of the insoluble enigma, together with the inevitability of death, that had come upon him that autumn evening when his brother had come to him . . . even less than before did he feel capable of apprehending the meaning of death."[8]

Levin's perplexity and doubt about the possibility of making sense of his life is compounded when he discovers that his wife Kitty is pregnant. Even before the death of his brother Levin is challenged to come to terms with another enigma, which makes the riddle of life more troubling and problematic than ever: "The one mystery of death, still unsolved, had scarcely passed before his eyes, when another mystery had arisen, as insoluble, urging him to love and to life."[9] In the weeks and months following the death of his brother, as Levin and Kitty anticipate the birth of their first child, Levin still finds it hard to come to terms with the sense of perplexity about the meaning of his life. In fact, when Kitty finally goes into labor, Levin rushes to fetch the doctor and is perplexed and bewildered when he suddenly begins to pray. In the midst of this spontaneous prayer, Levin discovers something new about his inner life which surprises him and forces him to reconsider his feelings about God: "At that instant he knew that all his doubts, even the impossibility of believing with his reason, of which he was aware in himself, did not in the least hinder his turning to God."[10] What is important to notice is that the intimations of religious faith we find here are partly the result of Levin's openness, his willingness to be surprised and challenged by a new way of understanding himself, and his vague understanding that any attempt to make sense of these strange new feelings and concerns may require another way of living.

What then has given rise to Levin's sense that the answer to his riddle might require another way of living? Part of the answer is Levin's realization that both his present joy over the birth of his child as well as the grief he experienced at the deathbed of his brother Nikolay point to something that calls into question his understanding of ordinary life. What Levin learns as he tries to make sense of these emotions and concerns is that the divine is revealed at the limits of our lives:

> Yet that grief and this joy were alike outside all the ordinary conditions of life; they were loopholes, as it were, in that ordinary life through which there came glimpses of something divine. And in the contemplation of this sublime something the soul was exalted to inconceivable heights of which it had before had no conception, while reason lagged behind, unable to keep up with it.[11]

It might, of course, be tempting to view Levin's religious experience here as the final crisis in his spiritual journey. However, as the story draws to a close we find that Levin is still wrestling with the questions that have preoccupied him throughout the novel. What fills Levin with horror, moreover, is not a fear of death but rather the impossibility of understanding life. Levin does realize, however, that the source of his perplexity is not a simple lack of knowledge. This is important because it serves to remind us that the religious view that follows from the attempt to make sense of one's life does not involve the acquisition of new information about the universe; instead it requires a willingness to acknowledge that one has become a riddle to oneself and that one's former ways of understanding oneself no longer appear to make sense. Thus, when Levin recalls his spontaneous prayers for his wife and child he is perplexed—he cannot make sense of such behavior in terms of his former self-understanding: "during his wife's confinement, something had happened that seemed extraordinary to him. He, an unbeliever, had fallen into praying, and at the moment he prayed, he believed. But that moment had passed, and he could not make his state of mind at that moment fit into the rest of his life."[12]

Levin's conversion therefore is largely a question of his desire to make that moment of prayer fit into the rest of his life. Moreover, his attempt to discover another way of understanding himself does not involve the acquisition of new information about the world nor does it involve some new philosophical insight. Levin's final discovery, rather, is to be found in what is ultimately an inexplicable transformation, a radical shift in his self-understanding that in turn opens up new possibilities for understanding life:

> What have I discovered? "I have discovered nothing. I have only found out what I knew. I understand the force that in the past gave me life, and now too gives me life. I have been set free from falsity, I have found the Master."[13]

Wittgenstein, who could have had Levin's conversion in mind while writing his own brief and enigmatic observations on the meaning of life, sums up quite nicely the nature of Levin's "discovery" when he observes in an early remark that the solution to the problem of life is the disappearance of the problem.[14] The answer has been found once the riddle has vanished.

Needless to say, much more can be said about Levin's spiritual quest. Suffice it to say, however, that throughout the story Levin is obsessed with the question of whether it is possible to make sense of his life as a whole. In the final analysis then, it might be best to characterize his discovery at the end of the novel not in terms of knowledge, for Levin himself admits that he has learned nothing new. Nor is it helpful to suggest that Levin is entitled to hold these beliefs because they are justified in some narrow epistemic sense. What we have here, rather, is a perfect example of what it means to say that the ethics of belief is primarily a question of critical self-reflection. To say that Levin's religious beliefs are "justified" is simply to say that he has discovered new possibilities for self-understanding that enable him to make sense out of his life as a whole.

B. *The Scope and Limits of Self-Understanding: Kierkegaard vs. Nietzsche*

Having seen how Levin's conversion is primarily a matter of arriving at a new way of understanding his life, it might be a good idea to say a few words about what I mean by self-understanding. First of all, it is important to remember that self-understanding is not primarily some kind of disinterested or theoretical knowledge that I have about my character and personality. Although such information provides me with some important insights about myself, such knowledge *about* my life is not yet self-knowledge. As D. W. Hamlyn reminds us, it is possible for people to know quite a lot about themselves without possessing self-knowledge.[15] But if the cultivation of self-knowledge is not primarily a matter of acquiring new information about oneself, what is it? According to Hamlyn, whose insights on this issue are much in keeping with the views of

Søren Kierkegaard, the cultivation of self-knowledge is primarily a *practical* activity. This means that self-knowledge demands much more than some type of contemplative understanding of oneself. Rather, the cultivation of self-knowledge requires a willingness to take responsibility for the person one is by actively endorsing one's ideals and commitments. As Hamlyn himself suggests: "The man who knows himself in this way . . . knows, without obscuring the fact from himself, where his values lie, what he truly wants, and where he stands in relation to those wants."[16] The cultivation of self-knowledge then requires what Søren Kierkegaard has called "subjective reflection," which is just another way of saying that self-knowledge involves the practical endorsement and appropriation of those basic projects and concerns that give shape and meaning to one's life:

> When the question of truth is raised in an objective manner, reflection is directed objectively to the truth, as an object to which the knower is related. Reflection is not focused upon the relationship, however, but upon the question of whether it is truth to which the knower is related. . . . When the question of the truth is raised subjectively, reflection is directed subjectively to the nature of the individual's relationship. . . .[17]

Much has been said about Kierkegaard's appeal to notions such as "subjective reflection" and both sympathizers and critics generally admit how difficult it is to make sense out of his more notorious claim that "truth is subjectivity." Although a detailed discussion of these troublesome issues is beyond the scope of this book, I think it is clear that Kierkegaard's enigmatic observations concerning subjectivity can be viewed as another way of suggesting that the ethics of belief is primarily a question of *practical* self-understanding.

Like Wittgenstein, Kierkegaard is wary of any attempt to reduce faith to an epistemological notion and suggests therefore that it is a mistake to explain it as a special case of true justified belief. For this reason, his position is much in keeping with my contention that the ethics of belief is not primarily an epistemological concern. Implicit in his practice of presenting various and competing "life-views" in literary forms such as novels, journals, and letters is his suspicion that assessing a life-view requires a more holistic approach. How though should we think about such existential proposals and how might we appropriate what we learn about life in such literature? The answer is to be found, I believe, in Kierkegaard's appeal to the notion of "subjective reflection" which can provide us with a basis for the alternative account of the ethics of belief I wish to defend.

First of all, Kierkegaard sees the task of becoming a self as a project that involves an attempt to make sense of one's life through the exploration and appropriation of various self-interpretations or categories of self-understanding. The "subjectively interested thinker" recognizes that the cultivation of this kind of practical self-understanding is an essential part of living a life. Since Kierkegaard acknowledges that there is a wide variety of ideals and concerns that can give shape and meaning to a person's life, it should come as no surprise that much of his writing is devoted to the careful exploration and criticism of these various "life-possibilities." In the first volume of *Either/Or*, for example, Kierkegaard assumes the persona of a young poet in order to provide his reader with an insightful psychological picture of the aesthetic mode of life. In the second part of this work, we have several long letters written by another one of Kierkegaard's pseudonyms, Judge Wilhelm, who argues that the attempt to make sense of one's life in aesthetic terms is riddled with contradictions and is for this reason bound to fail. Therefore, he argues that one can make much better sense of one's life by striving to understand oneself in ethical terms, a task that requires a willingness to become a civic self by attending to one's communual responsibilities. Finally, however, in his other, more religious writings, Kierkegaard suggests that even the ethical criteria for selfhood might be too vulnerable to render one's life livable. In this way, Kierkegaard invites his reader to entertain the possibility that one may not be able to make sense out of one's life unless one is willing to appropriate specifically Christian concepts, such as sin and faith, to interpret one's situation.

Although Kierkegaard is right to insist that the task of becoming a Christian is best understood as a commitment to achieve a certain kind of self-understanding by the practical appropriation of Christian concepts, he is mistaken to insist, as he sometimes does, that this must be regarded as the most authentic way of understanding oneself. Although Kierkegaard himself wants to refrain from these kinds of judgments in the pseudonymous works, many of his explicitly Christian writings seem to suggest that genuine self-knowledge is possible only for the believer who stands before God. In *The Sickness unto Death*, for example, Anti-Climacus, a pseudonym who expresses what is clearly a radically Christian perspective, insists that one attains the pure transparency of genuine self-understanding only through Christian faith. Throughout his discussion, Anti-Climacus maintains that all other attempts to achieve selfhood by appropriating human categories of self-understanding can only lead to despair. Although a detailed treatment of Anti-Climacus's difficult discussion would take us too far afield, his major concern stems from his suspicion that any attempt to secure the integrity of the self by an appeal to temporal or revisable criteria of self-understanding would be too vulnerable to secure our confidence. For if the integrity of a life depends on the possibility of self-knowledge, what is needed is an *unchangeable* criterion of self-understanding that might ensure the stability of the self. Fortunately, insists Anti-Climacus, this kind of *unchangeable* criterion of self-understanding is God and it is for this reason that he characterizes faith as the appropriation of what he calls a theological criterion for self-understanding:

> The formula that describes the state of the self when despair is completely rooted out is this: in relating itself to itself and in willing to be itself, the self rests transparently in the power that established it.[18]

Throughout his writings Kierkegaard wants to show that the realization of selfhood depends on the possibility of genuine self-understanding and that the threat of "opacity" therefore renders the self vulnerable to instability. This, I think, is one of the more interesting insights that inform Kierkegaard's reflections on selfhood. Clearly, he is keenly aware that the fragility of selfhood is a matter of the many ways our knowledge of ourselves can be put at risk, especially when our identities are intimately tied to earthly cares which themselves are fragile and vulnerable. The question then is whether there is any way to deal with the kind of anxiety that arises from this suspicion that the criteria for human self-understanding may be too changeable and uncertain to ensure the integrity of the self.

As I have already suggested, Kierkegaard maintains that there is a theological criterion of self-understanding that can secure the possibility for selfhood. In the collection of discourses collected under the title *Purity of Heart*, for instance, Kierkegaard insists that the basis for our confidence is nothing other than the Eternal: "Only the Eternal is always appropriate and always present, is always true. Only the Eternal applies to each human being, whatever his age may be."[19] As Kierkegaard stresses a little later in the discourse, the one who confesses comes before God not to inform God about something that God does not know, for God is omniscient. Instead, the very fact that God already knows everything in the heart of the one who confesses is grounds for our confidence that self-knowledge is possible: "Much that you are able to keep hidden in darkness, you first get to know by your opening it to the knowledge of the all-knowing One."[20] So although there may not be a way to demonstrate in some rigorous fashion that self-understanding is possible, the one who confesses to God can trust that self-understanding is a reality.

Kierkegaard addresses similar concerns throughout his edifying writings, but perhaps the most straightforward statement concerning the relationship between the Eternal and the possibility of self-understanding can be found in the discourse "Becoming Sober," published posthumously in 1876 as a part of *Judge for Yourselves!* In this short but challenging piece, Kierkegaard confronts an age that he sees as suffering from an intoxicating form of ignorance and self-deception. The challenge then is to become sober. But what does it mean to become sober? Once again, Kierkegaard insists that the remedy for this spiritual intoxication is knowledge, but qualifies his recommendation by claiming that "There is only one sort of knowledge which brings a man to himself entirely, and that is self-knowledge; this is what it is to be sober, the true transparency."[21]

Given Kierkegaard's concern for ensuring the stability of the self by an appeal to some unchanging and invulnerable criterion of self-understanding, it should come as no surprise to learn that he emphasizes the importance of self-examination before God. Again, it is clear that when Kierkegaard speaks of the true criterion of self-understanding that ensures the possibility of selfhood, he is anxious to distinguish this Christian form of self-examination from those forms of self-understanding that threaten to undermine the integrity of the self. Consider, for instance, the following observation from *Judge for Yourselves!*:

> To come to oneself is self-knowledge, *and before God*. For if self-knowledge does not lead to knowing oneself before God, then indeed there is something in what the merely human view says, that it leads to a certain emptiness which produces dizziness. Only by being before God can a man entirely come to himself in the transparency of sobriety.[22]

Unlike the human view of self-knowledge that leaves the self vulnerable to "a certain emptiness," self-knowledge *before God* secures the possibility for the kind of self-understanding required for the task of becoming a self. Thus, the individual who stands before God is transparent in sobriety and need not fear the existential vertigo that threatens to undermine the self.

In the end then, it is clear that any attempt to rethink the ethics of belief in terms of critical self-reflection poses some interesting questions concerning the possibility of self-understanding. As I have tried to show, Kierkegaard is right to suggest that the decision to become a Christian is best construed as a commitment to make sense of one's life by the subjective appropriation of Christian concepts of self-understanding. The task of Christian practice then involves the reshaping of one's life through a critical redescription of those self-interpretations that are constitutive of the self. Furthermore, Kierkegaard realizes that the task of becoming a self is complicated by the various ways a person's self-understanding can be challenged and put at risk. This is another way of saying that there is always a possibility that competing strategies for making sense of one's life might lead one to question one's present values and commitments.

As we have seen, however, Kierkegaard's explicitly Christian writings suggest that it is possible to safeguard the task of becoming a self by appealing to an unchanging criterion of self-understanding. It is important to stress, however, that Kierkegaard refuses to base his confidence in the theological criterion of selfhood on some kind of philosophical argument. In fact, his main objection to Hegel, I believe, stems from what he takes to be Hegel's mistaken belief that the possibility of self-knowledge can be assured by a philosophical argument that appeals to the Absolute. Kierkegaard is critical of such philosophical attempts to account for the possibility of self-knowledge. There is no transcendental deduction that can set our mind at ease. It is clear though that even though Kierkegaard is skeptical of any *philosophical* attempt to ensure the possibility of self-knowledge, he is confident that there is a *theological* basis for our confidence. In the end, says Kierkegaard, the Christian is confident that our lives can be rendered understandable and therefore livable to the extent that the Eternal provides a stable criterion that can ensure the integrity of the self. If the possibility of self-understanding is a matter of trust, it is a sense of trust based on a prior commitment and belief in the unchangeableness of God:

> Oh, in the unchangeableness of God there is rest! When you therefore permit this unchangeableness to serve you according to His will, for your own welfare; when you submit yourself to discipline, so that your selfish will (and it is from this that change chiefly comes, more than from the outside) dies away, the sooner the better . . . when you submit to be disciplined by his unchangeable will, so as to renounce inconstancy and changeableness and self-will: then you will steadily rest more and more securely, and more and more blessedly in the unchangeableness of God.[23]

I have already suggested that Kierkegaard's attempt to ensure a stable criterion of self-understanding by an appeal to the Eternal can be construed as an unacceptably stoic response to an otherwise valid insight. One cannot help but wonder whether the type of unconditional commitment that Kierkegaard sometimes recommends as the basis of faith may not in the end blind one to other possibilities for making sense of one's life. In those cases where a person discovers that he can no longer make his life intelligible in Christian terms this is particularly important and what is needed is a willingness to entertain and explore other ways of understanding one's life. In the end, to say that the ethics of be-lief is primarily a question of practical self-understanding is to admit that losing faith might not always be a bad thing and that our desire to make sense of our lives as a whole might require both the courage to abandon old ways of thinking about our lives as well as insight for the discovery of new "life-possibilities."

Although the task of becoming a self requires a willingness to en-gage in critical self-reflection, it is important to remember that there are limits to this type of activity. For this reason, I think that writers such as Friedrich Nietzsche are mistaken when they make the more radical suggestion that we should always be willing to test and abandon *all* of our fundamental commitments and projects. Nietzsche himself seems to think that the pursuit of intellectual honesty involves the cultivation of a kind of existential skepticism and that one should *always* be willing to call into question one's most cherished ideals and values. Consider, for example, the following passage from *Daybreak* in which Nietzsche advises Christians to take up an experimental attitude to their beliefs in order to determine whether their faith is genuine:

> The serious, excellent, upright, deeply sensitive people who are still Christians from the very heart: they owe it to themselves to try for once the experiment of living for some length of time without Christianity, they owe it to *their faith* in this way for once to sojourn 'in the wilderness'—if only to win for them-selves the right to a voice on the question of whether Christian-ity is necessary. For the present they cleave to their native soil and thence revile the world beyond it: indeed, they are provoked and grow angry if anyone gives them to understand that what lies beyond their native soil is the whole wide world! that Chris-tianity is, after all, only a little corner! No, your evidence will be of no weight until you have lived for years without Christian-ity, with an honest and fervent zeal to endure life in antithesis to Christianity: until you have wandered far, far away from it. Only if you are driven back, not by homesickness but by *judg-ment* on the basis of a rigorous *comparison*, will your home-coming possess any significance.[24]

The kind of "experimentalism" that Nietzsche recommends in *Day-break* and in his other works seems to be based on the mistaken view that it is desirable for people to test their basic cares and concerns by call-ing them into question in a radical way. Although there is something to be said for the cultivation of the type of honesty that Nietzsche himself values so highly, his proposal leads to some strange and rather troubling problems. Very simply, Nietzsche fails to consider the possibility that in some cases it makes no sense to question one's basic concerns in this radical kind of way.

Imagine, for example, a faithful husband who wants to know whether the love he feels for his wife is genuine. One way to test his affections is to follow Nietzsche's advice and subject his marriage to an "experiment." He may decide, for example, that the only way to determine whether he really loves his wife is to explore various extramarital relationships. Clearly, however, this is an unacceptable way of testing his marriage for the simple reason that there is no way to carry out his extramarital experiments without jeopardizing his love for his wife. In a similar way, I want to suggest that it is too much to ask religious believers to call into question all of their most fundamental religious values in order to see whether they are genuine. Even though the ethics of belief involves the cultivation of a certain kind of critical self-reflection, Nietzsche's austere appeal to the will-to-truth seems unacceptable. If Kierkegaard sometimes errs by failing to realize that an unconditional commitment to the cultivation of Christian self-understanding may blind a person to other ways of making sense of life, Nietzsche's approach to the ethics of belief opens the way to a kind of rootless skepticism that threatens to vitiate the very possibility of giving shape and meaning to one's life. Too much suspicion about our values and commitments is a bad thing.

Basically, the problem with the type of "experimentalism" that Nietzsche seems to recommend in *Daybreak* is the assumption that our basic projects and commitments are suspect unless we can defend them in some way. However, contemporary writers such as Bernard Williams have reminded us that this kind of assumption is misguided and that it does not make sense for a person to begin with the idea that his or her basic projects and concerns are in need of some kind of justification. In an insightful article entitled "Persons, Character, and Morality,"[25] for instance, Williams suggests that what gives shape and meaning to a person's life are what he calls "categorical desires." The important thing to note about these desires is that they reflect a commitment to those fundamental projects and concerns that make a person's life worth living. Williams, of course, is quite clear that these desires should not be construed in a narrow way and could express a wide variety of basic concerns. As he himself states, "the propelling concerns may be of a relatively everyday kind as certainly provide the ground for many sorts of happiness."[26] One's interest in one's family or one's commitment to one's career would be two good examples of certain kinds of desires that give shape and meaning to a person's life. In addition, because these are the basic concerns in terms of which a person makes sense of his or her life, it does not make sense to ask for some deeper or more fundamental concern to "justify" these ground projects.

Although Williams himself would probably be reluctant to admit that a person's religious commitments could be construed in this way,[27] I do not see how his account of categorical desires could rule out such a possibility. The point is that if a person's religious commitments can be construed as an example of this kind of basic concern, we would have good reason to reject the type of radical experimentalism proposed by Nietzsche. In Williams's view, this kind of experimentalism would be considered suspect precisely because it fails to take into account the possibility that a person's religious beliefs may be tied to such categorical desires.

It is important to stress, however, that although there is no prima facie reason for people to adopt this kind of experimental attitude toward their religious commitments, there is always the possibility that some legitimate concern might justify this kind of suspicion. The best example of this kind of possibility is raised by Nietzsche in his brilliant analysis of the ascetic ideal in his book *The Geneology of Morals* in which he explores the various ways ressentiment can inform a person's religious commitments. The point I want to stress, however, is that although it is a mistake to call our basic concerns and commitments into question in some arbitrary fashion, an analysis such as that offered by Nietzsche in *The Geneology of Morals* might give us legitimate reasons to seek some critical leverage with respect to our "categorical desires." Although his general suspicion of the Christian ethos is unwarranted, there might be specific cases in which there is much to be gained from this kind of "hermeneutics of suspicion."

If the ethics of belief is primarily a question of critical self-reflection, as I want to claim, then what is needed is some way to steer a path between two unacceptable approaches to the problem. On the one hand, if one's religious commitments are an expression of one's most basic concerns and projects, the extreme type of "experimentalism" that Nietzsche sometimes recommends is unacceptable. There are limits to practical self-understanding, and it is not desirable to begin with a radical suspicion that would lead us to question all of our concerns. One might even use a Kierkegaardian turn of phrase and say that the desire to put all of our cares at risk in this way is symptomatic of a contempt for our subjectivity.

On the other hand, people who are dogmatically committed to the cultivation of Christian self-understanding may sometimes discover that they can no longer make their lives intelligible in these terms and fail to realize or acknowledge this fact. There are, of course, many ways people might deal with this kind of situation. A person may attempt and succeed to some extent in rationalizing or redescribing certain concepts in order to preserve his or her Christian identity. There comes a point, however, when one might be tempted to maintain and nurture one's Christian identity long after there is no longer any connection between the way one leads one's life and the way one understands his or her life. When this happens, those very concepts that might have enabled the person to make sense of life at one time become an obstacle to genuine self-understanding. One who strives to preserve one's Christian identity at all costs might discover that one has become an engima to oneself and that life has simply become a "dark saying." It is for this reason that we need to account for those situations in which a person becomes a victim of an obsessive search to find meaning in a way of life that has long since become meaningless. In short, what we need to consider is the problem of self-deception.

Notes

1. This type of proposal is developed quite elegantly in connection with Nietzsche's writings by Alexander Nehamas in his *Nietzsche: Life as Literature* (Cambridge: Harvard University Press, 1985), esp. chapter 5.

2. Cited by J. Burnaby, *Amor Dei* (London: Hodder & Stoughton, 1938), p. 98.

3. Leo Tolstoy, *Anna Karenina*, trans. Constance Garnett (Indianapolis: Bobbs-Merrill, 1978).

4. Ibid., p. 297.

5. Ibid., p. 299.

6. Ibid., p. 487.

7. Ibid., pp. 379–80.

8. Ibid., p. 541.

9. Ibid., pp. 541–42.

10. Ibid., p. 756.

11. Ibid., p. 761.

12. Ibid., p. 838.

13. Ibid., p. 848.

14. Ludwig Wittgenstein, *Tractatus Logico-Philosophicus*, trans. D. F. Pears and B. F. McGuinness (London: Routledge and Kegan Paul, 1972), 6.521.

15. D. W. Hamlyn, "Self-Knowledge," in *Perception, Learning, and the Self: Essays in the Philosophy of Psychology* (London: Routledge and Kegan Paul, 1983), pp. 245–47.

16. Ibid., p. 250.

17. Søren Kierkegaard, *Concluding Unscientific Postscript*, trans. David F. Swenson and Walter Lowrie (Princeton: Princeton University Press, 1941), p. 178.

18. Søren Kierkegaard, *The Sickness unto Death*, ed. and trans. Howard and Edna Hong (Princeton: Princeton University Press, 1980), p. 14.

19. Søren Kierkegaard, *Purity of Heart Is to Will One Thing*, trans. Douglas V. Steere (New York: Harper and Row, 1956), p. 49.

20. Ibid., p. 51.

21. Søren Kierkegaard, *For Self-Examination and Judge for Yourselves!*, trans. and intro. Walter Lowrie (Princeton: Princeton University Press, 1944), p. 122.

22. Ibid.

23. Ibid., p. 238.

24. Friedrich Nietzsche, *Daybreak: Thoughts on the Prejudices of Morality*, trans. R. J. Hollingsdale (Cambridge: Cambridge University Press, 1982), p. 62.

25. Bernard Williams, *Moral Luck: Philosophical Papers 1973–1980* (Cambridge: Cambridge University Press, 1981), pp. 1–19.

26. Ibid., p. 12.

27. Williams himself gives a brief statement concerning his view on religion in his recent book, *Ethics and the Limits of Philosophy* (Cambridge: Harvard University Press, 1985), esp. pp. 32–33.

5

Self-Deception and the Ethics of Belief

Lying to oneself about oneself, deceiving oneself about the pretense in your own state of will, must have a harmful influence on (one's) style; for the result will be that you cannot tell what is genuine in the style and what is false. . . . If you are *unwilling* to know what you are, your writing is a form of deceit.

Working in philosophy—like work in architecture in many respects—is really more like working on oneself. On one's own interpretation. On one's own way of seeing things. . . . Nothing is so difficult as not deceiving oneself.

Ludwig Wittgenstein[1]

Although the notion of self-deception provides an important criterion for the assessment of a person's beliefs, emotions, and actions, it is a strange concept that draws our attention to one of the more perplexing dimensions of human life. One might even be tempted to say that this human capacity for illusion and self-deceit is precisely what makes the exploration of the inner life so interesting. Not surprisingly, because a consideration of self-deception tends to complicate our picture of the religious life, many philosophers of religion and theologians have, until recently, tended to ignore it. It is probably for this reason that the most sensitive and astute accounts of self-deception are to be found not in the writings of philosophers, but in the works of novelists, playwrights, and screenwriters. One only has to think of stories such as Tolstoy's *The Death of Ivan Ilych*, novels such as Dostoyevski's *The Brothers Karamazov* or Thomas Hardy's *Jude the Obscure*, and plays and movies such as Ibsen's *The Master Builder* and Ingmar Bergman's *Winter Light* to realize that a nuanced picture of illusion, deception, and delusion requires an artist's skill.

This is not to say, of course, that philosophers have had nothing to say about this topic. Kierkegaard, Nietzsche, and Sartre are just a few of the thinkers who have encouraged us to think about the complex strategies and tactics that enable us to avoid the truth about ourselves. And in recent years some analytical philosophers with an interest in philosophical psychology, philosophy of mind, and ethics have begun to take a fresh look at these issues.[2] Our question, however, is whether a consideration of the problem of self-deception can help enrich our understanding of what it means to assess a person's religious convictions.

A. *The Ethics of Self-Deception*

Despite my criticisms of Nietzsche in the last chapter, it is impossible to deny that what he calls "schooling in suspicion" is an essential part of the ethics of belief. Like all of Nietzsche's important insights, however, this sharp and incisive view is a sword that cuts both ways. On the one hand, he sometimes suggests that our lives are bearable only because we have the capacity to evade the truth, especially at those times in life when too much truth might undermine and erode those basic commitments that enable us to make sense of the world. In the "Preface" to his *Human, All Too Human*, Nietzsche addresses this theme when he offers his own somewhat ambivalent confession to rationalize his youthful enthusiasm for Schopenhauer and Wagner. Not surprisingly, he suggests that if there is any excuse for failing to see the failing of our avatars, it is because there is never any reason to ask for the *whole* truth when a little truth will suffice: " . . . what do *you* know, what *could* you know, of how much cunning in self-preservation, how much reason and higher safeguarding, is contained in such deception—or how much falsity I shall *require* if I am willing to permit myself the luxury of *my* truthfulness. . . . Enough, I am still living, and life is, after all, not a product of morality: it *wants* deception, it *lives* on deception. . . ."[3]

Although we cannot endorse the more radical implications of Nietzsche's "experimentalism," the challenge posed by his insights concerning religion and self-deception is inescapable. In the world according to Nietzsche, our lives are livable only because each person has an excuse for his or her illusions; namely, that a finite and limited perspective is what makes *human* life possible. And yet, even if we reject Nietzsche's "experimentalism," he does offer us an alternative ideal, what one might call the life of philosophical irony which is captured by his portrait of the "free spirit," the person who assumes the risks of inquiry even though it might lead to the erosion of his or her life-preserving deceptions. Anticipating the meditations of the "free spirit" offered in his later works, Nietzsche casts this ironical way of life as a "spiritual" journey and suggests that this sort of person suffers from an essential loneliness—a solitude and certain cold-hearted suspicion of oneself which is prelude to a kind of personal transformation: "You shall become master over yourself, master also over your virtues. . . ."[4]

Despite his more radical and unacceptable views then, I present these Nietzschean observations because I believe that they provide two fruitful alternatives for articulating the ethics of belief once we have embraced a nonfoundational picture of religious belief. Although the critique of foundationalism discussed earlier in connection with Locke has become something of a commonplace in many philosophical circles, few have yet acknowledged the far-reaching implications such a shift of perspective might have on the ethics of belief. As we have already seen, according to the traditional picture inherited from Locke, one is entitled to one's religious beliefs only if they can be justified by an appeal to neutral epistemic criteria such as truth and justifiedness. Romantic thinkers such as Coleridge and Newman reject this picture and offer an alternative which in recent years has inspired a more "pragmatic" approach that suggests that nothing of major importance turns on the distinction between epistemic and nonepistemic criteria for the assessment of a person's religious beliefs. According to this more radically nonfoundational picture, there is no reason why epistemic criteria should be given more weight than other considerations that might be relevant for assessing a person's religious convictions.

I do not want to deny that this approach to the ethics of belief does not pose some challenges of its own. In particular, I believe that such a proposal must acknowledge the Nietzschean challenge and address the question of whether the kind of self-manipulations that enable a person to cultivate and preserve his or her basic commitments sometimes involve some form of self-deception. According to the traditional picture, of course, illicit strategies for preserving one's beliefs are said to involve simple epistemic failures, such as a refusal to entertain objections or systematic attempts to ignore relevant evidence inimical to one's beliefs. More interesting, however, are those more subtle strategies for maintaining one's religious beliefs which remain hidden from view, if only because they are accepted as normal and defensible ways of preserving the stability of one's particular way of construing the world. Although it might be false to say that a person is able to choose his or her basic cares and commitments by a sheer act of will, this volitionalist fallacy should not blind us to the fact that many of our everyday decisions are motivated in part by a desire to foster and protect our life-views. As Harry

Frankfurt has recently argued, not only do persons have cares, they also have second-order cares that enable them to care for and cultivate their first-order cares.[5]

At this point I want to stress that there is nothing a fortiori objectionable to the kind of self-manipulations that are sometimes required for the preservation of one's commitments. Unless one is a purist and holds a hyperrationalistic view of rationality that rules out such strategies as concessions to intellectual chaos, there is no reason to reject modest forms of self-manipulation as morally blameworthy. Some thinkers, such as Jon Elster, for example, have suggested that far from being concessions to irrationality, strategies such as "binding oneself" or "character planning" might actually be ways of compensating for failures of rationality such as weakness of the will.[6] Even though Elster is less sanguine about such possibilities in his later writings,[7] in which he notes that many such strategies can be self-defeating, he still acknowledges that they might still play some role in rationalizing our basic commitments and concerns.

What, however, is the relationship between doxastic self-manipulation and self-deception? Even if we were willing to grant a limited role to the types of self-manipulation that might enable believers to preserve their commitments, this still does not advance the stronger thesis, found in Nietzsche's work, that self-deception might be an unavoidable trait of our species, given our human, all too human, need to protect our basic commitments. To make sense of this stronger claim, it might be helpful to examine briefly some observations made by Amelie Rorty that may illuminate the problem.

According to Rorty, the reason why traditional accounts of agency cannot accommodate notions such as self-deception and weakness of the will is that they tend to presuppose a rather centralized notion of the self.[8] Rorty appeals to a metaphor made famous by Wittgenstein in his discussion of language and suggests that if we view the self as a city, traditional models will appear as maps organized according to uniform and preplanned principles. In order to get a better idea of how self-deception is possible, Rorty invites us to shift our perspective of the self and imagine that this rather centralized city has been superimposed on the map of an ancient medieval town which, unlike the modern city, is more loosely organized. The task then is to try and understand how the interrelationship between these two "maps" might yield an acceptable model of the self that would also allow for self-deception.

What makes Rorty's discussion relevant for our purposes is her suggestion that even though we cannot abandon the view that integrity is the fundamental goal of selfhood, we should acknowledge the possibility that the divided self might be the natural expression of what it means to be a person. First of all, she notes that the task of becoming a self requires certain habits, skills, and capacities that cannot easily be reconciled. On the one hand, selfhood requires a certain unity of character and a practical self-confidence that secures the stability of those basic commitments that make life meaningful. By the same token, however, a person needs to acquire a certain flexibility characterized by an ability to view one's basic commitments from a critical perspective and to acknowledge the possibility of competing possibilities for making sense of one's life. An analogous conflict emerges when we examine the dialectical tension that characterizes the relationship between the community and the individual. In this regard, the fact that a person cannot acquire his basic commitments de novo leads Rorty to claim that the cultivation of these concerns requires what she calls "empathy," even though such a basic disposition is likely to conflict at times with the equal but competing claims of the individual's quest for "autonomy."[9] Given this Rousseauian picture of the conditions necessary to become a full-fledged self, it should come as no surprise that the integrity of the self is never simply a given, but remains a task to be achieved.

At this point I should mention that I have chosen Rorty's account because her appeal to the divided self illuminates, in a way other accounts do not, Nietzsche's claim that self-deception may be an unavoidable strategy for maintaining personal integrity. Of particular importance is her assumption that there is no hard and fast distinction between modest forms of self-manipulation and self-deception per se. Although analytic philosophers interested in self-deception have tended to focus on the hard cases that appear to involve a paradox[10]—namely, whether it is possible to lie to oneself or hold contradictory beliefs about the same thing—I have chosen Rorty's account because it avoids the conceptual difficulties of traditional accounts. For instead of presupposing an overly rationalistic picture of agency in light of which self-deception looks like a problematic aberration, Rorty begins with self-deception as the given and asks what kind of picture of agency it entails.

Rorty's insights then should lead us to suspect that the preservation of one's religious commitments poses some interesting challenges that trade on her understanding of the divided self. This is especially true in a pluralistic context in which competing ways of making sense of life present one with a wide range of opportunities for attaining some critical leverage with respect to one's religious beliefs. It is important to stress, of course, that such a scenario need not necessarily lead to the erosion of one's beliefs. The point, rather, is that the conflicting claims of practical self-confidence and critical flexibility or the opposing demands for empathy and autonomy make it increasingly difficult to cultivate and sustain one's religious beliefs without succumbing to the temptation of self-deception.

If we return for a moment to the Nietzschean observations with which I began this discussion, I think it should be clear that his "schooling in suspicion" allows for two different but equally understandable responses to the kind of dilemma posed by Rorty's discussion. On the one hand, Nietzsche acknowledges that self-deception might play an important role in the economy of selfhood. For if we admit that a person's religious beliefs are intimately connected to those self-constitutive concerns in terms of which he or she makes sense of life, and acknowledge that there is no reason to expect that a person will always be able to reconcile conflicts when these basic concerns are called into question, we should not be surprised that self-deception becomes an important strategy for the preservation of one's religious identity.

Self-deception then is not always an unacceptable alternative for theists struggling to maintain their faith in the face of the challenges that threaten to erode it. If Rorty is right, the traditional picture that reduces self-deception to a species of irrationality oversimplifies the complex ways this perplexing strategy serves a rational function by securing the stability of our psychic economy. The problem that Rorty herself wants to acknowledge, however, is that even though self-deception might be an acceptable strategy for preserving one's identity in the face of competing commitments, it is a strategy one cannot consciously adopt. As she maintains, a person cannot "himself choose that course under a description that justifies it."[11] This remark, it seems to me, is perfectly consistent with our ordinary intuitions about self-deception and confirms our sense that although it is a criterion of appraisal that we often invoke to excuse another person's failure in judgment, we do not ordinarily invoke it to excuse ourselves, unless, of course, we are speaking of the past. The peculiar nature of a comment such as "Oh, you must forgive me, I must be self-deceived" reveals something important about the conditions for ascribing self-deception to someone.

For the most part, I think that there is something to be said for Rorty's general suggestion that self-deception may not always be wrong and that "the strongly righteous determination to wipe out self-deception and *akrasia* can sometimes lead to strong vice."[12] The problem with this proposal, however, is that even though self-deception, considered on its own terms, may not always be a vice, the Christian tradition at least has always seemed to identify it as a spiritual flaw or failing. This tendency to view self-deception in moralistic terms is tied, I believe, to a particular tradition according to which self-deception is motivated by an unwillingness to acknowledge one's sin. As Søren Kierkegaard reminds us throughout his later writings, human beings are quite skillful in devising elaborate strategies to evade the fact that they are rebels against God. According to this picture, self-deception is always wrong for the simple reason that it is an expression of sinful defiance.

Not surprisingly then the suggestion that self-deception is not necessarily a moral species and is sometimes required for the preservation of faith may seem quite odd to the Christian who identifies self-deception with sin. On this Augustinian view, sin is the term used to describe the condition of the self divided against itself which must devise self-deceptive strategies to preserve the illusion of integrity. The opposite of this ersatz transparency, according to this view, is faith—the true integrity of the self who stands before God.

The problem though is whether the difference between the illusory integrity of sin and the genuine integrity of faith is overdrawn, even on the Christian's own terms. Consider, for instance, the classic Kierkegaardian dilemma. In his magnificent attempt to explore the moral and religious perplexity of Abraham as he leads his son Isaac up Mount Moriah for sacrifice, Kierkegaard's pseudonym Johannes de Silentio insists that one distinguishing characteristic of the knight of faith is his inability to reconcile two conflicting and incommensurable ways of understanding himself. On the one hand, he is the father of Isaac, bound to his son by natural ties of affection and obligation. On the other hand, insists de Silentio, Abraham understands himself as God's faithful servant, bound to obey by virtue of his unconditional loyalty. On de Silentio's reading, to understand faith would be to understand how a single person might be able to reconcile a father's love for his son with God's terrible, almost unspeakable, demand. The question is simple: In what sense can Abraham's act of faith possibly be construed as the expression of faithful integrity?

This question, I think, is the central concern in *Fear and Trembling*. The focus is not simply on whether Abraham will get Isaac back—with God all things are possible. The real concern of the knight of faith is whether he can carry out the command and get himself back in one piece. What intensifies the pathos of the knight of faith, then, who knows more than anyone that conflicting self-interpretations render his life a veritable enigma, is the hope that there might be a story that makes sense of this whole dreadful scenario. De Silentio, of course, tries and fails in the wonderful prelude with which the book begins—and yet, the desire for integrity leads us to hope that there still is a story that will unify this life and render it intelligible. After all, with God, all things are possible.

What moral should we draw from this Kierkegaardian meditation? In the end, I think the question of whether Abraham's act of faith is an act of integrity will depend on how we construe the suggestion that for

God all things are possible. From our perspective, of course, the question is whether the knight of faith can perform this act without sacrificing his integrity. But as de Silentio seems to suggest, the knight himself might view things differently as he desperately clings to the belief that this act of obedience is the *only* way to preserve it. And yet, we might secretly suspect that the claim—for God all things are possible—might turn out to be a rationalization to placate a self that quite understandably wants to preserve its unity. What is the final verdict? Either Abraham is a knight of faith or he is a self-deceiving murderer who appeals to the promise "for God all things are possible" as a simple rationalization to make sense of what appears to be a senseless act.

Even Kierkegaard sometimes seems to acknowledge the fine, almost invisible line separating true faith from self-deception. But perhaps this is inevitable, given what we have learned from Rorty's remarks. As Rorty rightly observes, the divided self and the possibility of self-deception become concerns only for the individual who already takes seriously the quest for spiritual integrity: "It is only when an agent takes the unification of his traits, his thoughts and his actions, as a central project that he is capable of self-deception and *akrasia*."[13] There is, of course, more than a bit of irony in the suggestion that it is the very desire to view one's life as an integrated whole that leads one to engage in the subtle strategies we usually associate with self-deception. But if this is the case, then perhaps we should reformulate our understanding of the dynamics of self-knowledge to allow for the subtle and nuanced relationship between "the multiple self" and the ideal of personal unity.

Needless to say, even though this kind of reformulation might provide us with a more nuanced account of the religious life, it also complicates the picture. For one thing, the believer cannot avoid the possibility that competing commitments and priorities may put his or her faith at risk and eventually lead to its erosion. From time to time, for example, when one feels spiritually vulnerable, one might find it necessary to engage in subtle strategies to protect one's religious life-view. In this regard, Pascal's advice to the unbeliever might be of more use to the borderline believer who needs to endure the dark night of the soul. Masses and holy water will probably not produce belief in an atheist, but perhaps they can help salvage it in the doubtful disciple. This is not to say, of course, that such strategies will be deliberate or conscious. This is especially the case when more modest forms of self-manipulation blossom into full-fledged cases of self-deception. When this occurs it might be necessary to invoke the peculiar but, I think, perfectly defensible notion of an "unconscious intention" to explain how such things might be possible. In any case, there is something to be said for the believer's understandable, if not always excusable, appeal to the faith-preserving strategy of self-deception.

B. *Doubt and Self-Deception in Ingmar Bergman's* Winter Light

Now that we have addressed the problems raised by the notion of self-deception and have explored one of the more plausible accounts of this notion, we are now in a better position to ask how a consideration of self-deception can enrich our understanding of the ethics of belief. As already mentioned, the assessment of people's religious beliefs involves the question of whether or not they truthfully avow their beliefs, desires, and intentions. If this is the case, then self-deception would be a good way to characterize either those situations in which one refuses to acknowledge beliefs, desires, or intentions that one actually holds *or* those situations in which one deliberately attributes to oneself beliefs, desires, or intentions one does not possess.

The most simple illustration of this kind of failure or refusal is the case of those individuals who insist that they believe God exists even though they do not in fact hold this belief. In cases such as this, for instance, we could appeal to the notion of self-deception when we suspect that the person in question intentionally refuses to acknowledge that he or she no longer believes in God. Of course, it is also possible to imagine a situation where one claims to be an atheist even though one really does believe in God. Although this possibility sounds a bit strange, it is one to which Kierkegaard draws our attention in *The Sickness unto Death*, in which his pseudonym Anti-Climacus maintains that it is precisely this kind of self-deception that characterizes the sin of despair.

Another interesting illustration of the way self-deception can help enrich the ways we assess a person's religious commitments is the case where one either ascribes emotions to oneself that one does not really feel or refuses to acknowledge one's true emotions. Considerations such as these are especially important in the context of the religious life where certain kinds of emotions such as guilt, sorrow, and joy, to name just a few, play such a central role in the life of the individual and the community. It is perhaps for this reason that a Christian writer such as Jonathan Edwards devotes so much painstaking care to an analysis of such emotions in his classic work, *The Religious Affections*. Although we can never hope to do justice to Edwards's amazing achievement in this book, it can serve to remind us that the possibility of self-deceptive emotions adds another dimension to the ethics of belief.

From the little that I have said so far, I hope it is clear that any attempt to do justice to the ethics of belief must come to terms with the many ways a person can refuse to acknowledge or feign certain religious beliefs or emotions. At this point though we need to remind ourselves of the simple fact that self-deception does not happen by accident. Self-deception is the way we characterize those *intentional* strategies people employ to evade the truth about themselves, even though such intentions are generally unconscious. But if it is indeed the case that self-deception is an intentional activity, then its usefulness as a criterion for assessing a person's beliefs, desires, and intentions depends on our ability to identify the possible *motivations* that might underlie the intention to deceive oneself. And the best way to understand such motivations is to view them in the context of a person's life story.

In his film *Winter Light*, for example, Ingmar Bergman offers us a fascinating psychological study of a Swedish minister, Tomas Erikson, whose struggle to come to terms with his own crisis of faith highlights the complex relationship between religious doubt and self-deception. After a regular Sunday service that takes place in a bleak and barren medieval church on a snowy November day, Tomas has a series of encounters with several members of the congregation that include a fisherman, Jonas Persson, and his wife Karin, as well as Marta Lundberg, a local schoolteacher. As the plot unfolds, we learn that Tomas is a widower and that the death of his wife has undermined the sense of security that had been the basis of his faith. Even though Tomas suspects that he can no longer make sense of his life in Christian terms, he refuses to acknowledge this fact. Instead of acknowledging his despair, he deceives himself by desperately clinging to the memory of his wife and a forgotten sense of vocation.

Early in the film, for example, we learn that the fisherman Jonas has been plagued by doubts and suicidal tendencies and has been encouraged by his wife Karin to seek spiritual counsel from Tomas. During their conversation, however, it is Tomas who confesses his religious doubts to Jonas. Tomas understands the basis of Jonas's despair but when he attempts to convey his sympathy with the young man's plight, he merely betrays his own lack of faith:

> When I was ordained I was as innocent as a babe in arms. Then everything happened at once. For a while I was seaman's pastor in Lisbon. It was during the Spanish Civil War. We had a front seat in the stalls. But I refused to see, or understand. I refused to accept reality. I and my God lived in one world, a specially arranged world, where everything made sense. All round were the agonies of real life. But I didn't see them. I turned my gaze toward God.[14]

Tomas continues his confession and admits that his decision to become a minister was motivated not by any genuine sense of vocation but rather by a desire to please his parents, whom he characterizes as "religious, pious, in a deep and natural way."[15] The motivation behind this observation is clear: Tomas wants to draw a sharp contrast between this kind of deep and natural faith, which he clearly acknowledges as a genuine possibility, and his own counterfeit belief. Furthermore, Tomas betrays the self-deceptive character of his faith when he admits that his interest in cultivating and ensuring the integrity of his Christian identity was based not on any genuine love of God, but rather on his desire for security. Perhaps we might even say that Tomas's faith is inauthentic precisely because it has been based on his refusal to acknowledge the vulnerability and fragility of his basic loves and concerns. As he admits: "I became a clergyman and believed in God. . . . A god who guaranteed me every imaginable security. Against fear of death. Against fear of life."[16]

Tomas's inability to come to terms with his crisis of faith is complicated by his relationship with Marta Lundberg, a middle-aged school teacher who wants to marry him. As the film unfolds we learn that even though Tomas and Marta have been lovers, Tomas is still captive to the memory of his dead wife and responds to Marta's marriage proposal with contempt. In a cruel outburst of emotion, Tomas not only tells Marta that he has never loved her, but insists that he has always found her habits and physical appearance to be repulsive. It is clear, however, that if Tomas does indeed find Marta intolerable, it is not because of her appearance, but because she poses a threat to his fragile and illusory world. On the one hand, when Marta voices her desire for marriage, Tomas is forced to face his inability to come to terms with his wife's death. Like his belief in God, Tomas's relationship with his wife seems to have been based on his need for security. For this reason, Tomas finds it difficult to imagine how his life could ever be meaningful again after the loss of his wife, but refuses to admit this to himself. In the end, Marta's interest in marriage serves as a painful reminder of Tomas's inability to face the truth about himself.

What is more troubling to Tomas, however, is the fact that Marta openly describes herself as an atheist and thereby reminds him of his own failure to come to terms with his lack of genuine religious faith. On one level, of course, Tomas knows that he has lost his faith. As we have already seen, when Jonas comes to Tomas for spiritual encouragement, Tomas confesses to Jonas that he too has been plagued by serious religious doubts. At one point he even makes the blasphemous admission that life is a riddle only for the person who believes in God. When, for example, Tomas asks what difference it would make if God does not exist, he offers the following answer:

> Life becomes something we can understand. What a relief! And death—extinction, dissolution of body and soul. People's cruelty, their loneliness, their fear—everything becomes self-evident—transparent.[17]

In our brief discussion of Tolstoy's *Anna Karenina* we explored Levin's spiritual journey and suggested that his belief in God arises primarily from his attempt to make sense out of his life as a whole. Like Tomas, Levin is bewildered by the problems of death, suffering, and evil and longs to find an answer that would enable him to understand life. But whereas Levin concludes that the answer to the enigma is belief in God, Tomas suspects that life might be more intelligible to the person who *does not* believe that God exists.

Unfortunately, although Tomas is vaguely aware that his Christian beliefs no longer enable him to understand life, he refuses to give them up and obstinately struggles to preserve the last vestige of his Christian identity. I would like to suggest that the hostility that Tomas feels toward Marta arises in part from a sense of resentment: she manages to acknowledge that she is an atheist while he cannot come to terms with his loss of faith. Marta is a threat to Tomas because she challenges him to confront the painful truth that he is clinging to a way of life that no longer makes any sense. In the end, Tomas seems to realize that he can no longer make sense of his life in Christian terms, but he refuses to acknowledge this fact. He is, in short, a victim of self-deception.

Bergman himself has characterized this film as a " 'reduction'—in the metaphysical sense of that word" and has subtitled the piece "certainty unmasked."[18] Unfortunately, this brief enigmatic remark does not shed too much light on the ambiguous ending of the film. As it turns out, Jonas commits suicide and Tomas returns to minister to his congregation only to find that the church is virtually empty. Although it looks as if the service might be canceled, Tomas approaches the altar and begins to pray as Marta offers her own prayer to her "silent god":

> If I could only lead him out of his emptiness, away from his lie-god. If we could dare to show each other tenderness. If we could believe in a truth. . . . If we could believe. . . .[19]

Marta's prayer is ambiguous and leaves room for differing conclusions about God's silence. The Christian would insist that what the atheist characterizes as the margins of unbelief is simply the dark night of the soul. On this view, even though Marta describes herself as an atheist, her "prayer" would seem to betray some kind of religious concern. One could even appeal to Simone Weil's observations concerning the "atheism of purification" and suggest that in some sense Marta's religious atheism is more genuine than Tomas's "spider god." According to this Christian interpretation then, what Tomas needs to acknowledge is that his life has been based on an inauthentic belief in a false god. But even on this Christian view, the film's ending remains ambiguous: even if Tomas were able to renounce his "spider god" we are still left with the question of whether genuine faith is a real possibility for him.

Bergman's film does provide us with some important insights regarding the complex and subtle ways the notion of self-deception contributes to our assessment of a person's religious convictions. First of all, Tomas's religious crisis reminds us how easily the basic commitments and desires that constitute a person's sense of identity can be challenged and undermined. More importantly, however, Tomas's response to his crisis demonstrates that self-deception can be motivated by a refusal to acknowledge that one's religious identity has been put at risk. In this case, Tomas's self-deception is motivated by his desire to secure the integrity of the self even though it means clinging to a way of life that he can no longer understand. So even if self-deception is not always blameworthy, it does exact a price: the pursuit of an illusory sense of security at the expense of becoming an enigma to oneself.

Notes

1. The first quotation is from Rush Rhees, ed., *Recollections of Wittgenstein* (New York: Oxford University Press, 1984), p. 174. The second quotation is from *Culture and Value*, ed. G. H. von Wright, trans. Peter Winch (Chicago: University of Chicago Press, 1977), p. 34e.

2. For an excellent introductory overview of the subject see Mike Martin, *Self-Deception and Morality* (Lawrence: University of Kansas Press, 1986). Other important and illuminating discussions of the topic include M. R. Haight, *A Study of Self-Deception* (Atlantic Highlands: Humanities Press, 1980); Ilham Dilman and D. Z. Phillips, *Sense and Delusion* (Atlantic Highlands: Humanities Press, 1971); Jon Elster, *Sour Grapes: Studies in the Subversion of Rationality* (Cambridge: Cambridge University Press, 1983); Herbert Fingarette, *Self-Deception* (Atlantic Highlands: Humanities Press, 1969); and David Pears, *Motivated Irrationality* (New York: Oxford University Press, 1984). Two relatively recent anthologies that contain a number of important essays are Mike Martin, ed., *Self-Deception and Self-Understanding: New Essays in Philosophy and Psychology* (Lawrence: University of Kansas Press, 1985) and Brian P. McLaughlin and Amelie Oksenberg Rorty, eds., *Perspectives on Self-Deception* (Berkeley: University of California Press, 1988).

3. Friedrich Nietzsche, *Human, All Too Human: A Book for Free Spirits*, trans. R. J. Hollingdale, intro. Erich Heller (Cambridge: Cambridge University Press, 1986), p. 6.

4. Ibid., p. 9.

5. Harry Frankfurt, "Freedom of the Will and the Concept of the Person," in *The Importance of What We Care About: Philosophical Essays* (Cambridge: Cambridge University Press, 1988), pp. 11–25.

6. See especially Jon Elster's *Ulysses and the Sirens: Studies in Rationality and Irrationality* (Cambridge: Cambridge University Press, 1984), chapter 2, which provides an enlightening and entertaining discussion of these issues.

7. Elster, *Sour Grapes: Studies in the Subversion of Rationality.*

8. Amelie Oksenberg Rorty, "Self-Deception, Akrasia, and Irrationality," in *The Multiple Self*, ed. Jon Elster (Cambridge: Cambridge University Press, 1987), pp. 115–31.

9. Ibid., p. 119ff.

10. One of the first articles to address the problem of self-deception in these terms was Raphael Demos, "Lying to Oneself," *Journal of Philosophy* 57 (1960): pp. 588–95.

11. Rorty, "Self-Deception, Akrasia, and Irrationality," p. 129.

12. Ibid.

13. Ibid., p. 131.

14. "Winter Light" in *Three Films by Ingmar Bergman*, trans. Paul Britten Austin (New York: Grove Press, 1967), p. 84.

15. Ibid.

16. Ibid., pp. 84–85.

17. Ibid., p. 86.

18. Ibid., p. 7.

19. Ibid., p. 104.

6

The Fragility of Faith

Human thought is unable to acknowledge the reality of
affliction. To acknowledge affliction means saying to oneself:
"I may lose at any moment, through the play of circumstances
over which I have no control, anything whatsoever I possess,
including those things which are so intimately mine that I
consider them as being myself. There is nothing that I might
not lose."

Simone Weil[1]

Any consideration of the ethics of belief must begin with one exploring the relationship between religious beliefs and the attempt to
understand oneself in light of basic questions and concerns about the
meaning of life. In the case of someone such as Konstantin Levin, whose
spiritual journey is described by Tolstoy in *Anna Karenina*, the struggle
to answer such basic questions leads to a realization that belief in God
renders life meaningful and transparent. However, this is not always the
case. Sometimes a person, such as Tomas Erikson in Bergman's *Winter
Light*, discovers that far from making life understandable, religious belief reduces everything to an obscure enigma. When this happens, one
can attempt to evade the problem of moral and spiritual perplexity by redescribing one's religious beliefs in such a way as to make sense of one's
life. However, there is no guarantee that this kind of bootstrapping will
be successful. In such cases, the spiritual prognosis is often poor: the person either succumbs to self-deception or a loss of faith.

In this chapter I want to suggest that much can be gained from a
closer examination of the many ways a person's belief can be put at risk
and undermined, in spite of the fact that philosophers of religion have

traditionally devised subtle and complex strategies to enable them to evade this problem. Philosophers of religion can learn an important lesson from Simone Weil, who rightly observes that the life of faith is always a difficult thing, especially when we attend to such inescapable problems as the possibility of suffering and affliction. The paradox, of course, is that even though the problems of evil, suffering, and death pose the kinds of questions for which religious faith might be an answer, they also present the kind of challenge that can sometimes lead to the erosion of faith. Unfortunately, however, there are many philosophers of religion who labor under the illusion that it is possible to justify the life of faith without taking such difficulties into account. I suspect, however, that the apparent success of such apologetic strategies is due to a refusal to acknowledge the fragility of faith.[2] In particular, although the picture of rationality that currently goes by the name of Reformed epistemology might establish that a person is within his or her epistemic rights to believe propositions such as "God exists," it fails to do justice to Weil's insight concerning the vulnerability of a person's religious identity. In their zeal to specify the minimal conditions under which it is *permissible* to hold a particular religious belief, the Reformed epistemologists fail to acknowledge the extent to which a loss of faith is tied to the many ways a person's religious identity can be put at risk.

A. *Toward a Critique of Reformed Epistemology*

Perhaps the best representative of what is called Reformed epistemology is Alvin Plantinga, whose most comprehensive presentation of his position can be found in his essay "Reason and Belief in God."[3] According to Plantinga, traditional challenges to theism are suspect to the extent that they rest on what he considers to be two undefensible philosophical dogmas: evidentialism and classical foundationalism. As we have seen, according to evidentialists such as John Locke, there is a presumption of atheism which entails that a person is not entitled to believe in the existence of God unless evidence can be offered to support this belief. With respect to this claim, Plantinga wonders whether there is something presumptuous about this presumption of atheism. Why not begin with the presumption that God exists? Perhaps part of the motivation behind the presumption of atheism is the assumption that belief in God is not a basic belief and must therefore be supported by beliefs that are "foundational." But this assumption too, argues Plantinga, is based on an indefensible epistemological position; namely, classical foundationalism. For the classical foundationalist, a person is within his or her epistemic rights to hold a belief only if the belief is properly basic—that is, self-evident, incorrigible, or evident to the senses—or if the belief can be supported in some fashion by an appeal to beliefs that are basic. Now the problem with classical foundationalism, Plantinga maintains, is that this criterion for appraising the acceptability of a person's beliefs is too narrow. In fact, the classical foundationalist's criterion for assessing beliefs is so narrow that it cannot account for the defensibility of the foundationalist criterion itself. Is the foundationalist criterion a properly basic belief; that is, is it self-evident, incorrigible, or evident to the senses? On the face of it, the classical foundationalist would be hard pressed to defend this claim. Of course, the classical foundationalist may respond with the claim that although the criterion is not properly basic, it can be supported by an appeal to beliefs that *are* basic. Plantinga, however, doubts the cogency of this response and argues that no such defense of the foundationalist's criterion is possible. Thus, in an argument very similar to the refutation of verificationism, Plantinga concludes that the foundationalist's position is incoherent: it is so narrow that the criterion itself cannot be justified.

The point, of course, is that there is no way to rule a priori what can and cannot be admitted as a properly basic belief. As Plantinga suggests, everyone has properly basic beliefs for which we can provide no evidence. Most of us believe in the existence of other minds and the external world, even though we would be hard pressed to provide evidence for these beliefs. What is of major importance to Plantinga, however, is the apologetic significance of his views concerning proper basicality. For if we accept Plantinga's more flexible view of what can be admitted as a properly basic belief, there is no reason to reject his suggestion that belief in God is properly basic. Of course, it is now easy to see why this more flexible understanding of proper basicality undermines the evidentialist's objections to theism. As already mentioned, the evidentialist believes that there is a presumption of atheism and that a person is not within his or her epistemic rights to believe in God without sufficient evidence or proof. Plantinga's position, however, calls this presumption into question; for if belief in God is properly basic then it makes no sense to ask for evidence or proof to justify this belief.

Needless to say, Plantinga's proposal has generated much controversy and debate, especially among those who suspect him of fideism. Such objections are based on the fear that Plantinga's account does not do justice to why someone might lose his or her belief in God. If, for example, one presses the analogy between the belief that God exists and other properly basic beliefs such as the belief in other minds or the existence of the external world, one might be tempted to conclude that belief in God has some type of privileged status. After all, it is hard to imagine what it might mean to give up one's belief in other minds or one's belief in the external world. Could it be that belief in God has a similar status for the believer? On the face of it, it would appear that there is an important disanalogy here: most sane people could not do without a belief in other minds whereas it is clear that there are in fact many normal human beings who get on perfectly well without belief in God. If belief in God is properly basic, it clearly is not properly basic for everyone.

It is important to point out that Plantinga himself is aware of this disanalogy and argues that although theistic belief is properly basic, there is a legitimate place for debate between theists and atheists; that is to say, it is possible to accept the proposition "God exists" without espousing a dogmatic attitude that refuses to entertain and respond to relevant objections. As Plantinga himself insists, although theists cannot provide evidence to support their beliefs, they can and should appeal to justifying circumstances. But since justification-conferring circumstances are prima facie rather than ultima facie, it is possible that a "defeater" might override a person's belief.[4] Of course, it is important to remember that potential defeaters can themselves be overridden by defeater defeaters, and so on. Thus, Plantinga concludes that a commitment to the proper basicality of theistic belief is perfectly compatible with a commitment to fallibilism.

It is clear then that Plantinga must allow for a kind of epistemic fallibilism, otherwise he could not make sense of the fact that argument sometimes undermines a person's belief in God. The question, however, is whether a purely epistemic approach to fallibilism does justice to the dramatic character of the religious life. The main problem is that Plantinga still wants to treat the ethics of belief as a primarily epistemological problem, and therefore only succeeds in showing that it is permissible for a person to believe in God without evidence. As I have suggested throughout this essay, however, a whole host of other issues connected with the ethics of belief require a more holistic approach to the problem and Plantinga's rather minimal proposal leaves too many issues unexplored.

One might wonder, for example, about those people who lose their faith not because of a failure to meet the atheist's objection with an appropriate defeater but because their lives change in such a way that they can no longer see the point in it. My suspicion is that when we speak about what it means for a person to lose faith, there is a tendency to forget the extent to which such a loss of faith is tied to changes in a person's perspective as a whole. We seem to think that when one abandons or loses one's religious beliefs, the reasons can be articulated independently of that person's entire life-view. According to a view such as Plantinga's, we might be tempted to assume that the person who loses his faith loses it because he cannot offer a convincing response to the atheist's objections. As Friedrich Nietzsche reminds us, however, this atomistic reduction of what counts either for or against our most important beliefs is apt to mislead. Consider, for example, the following brief observation from *The Gay Science*:

> Now something that you formerly loved as a truth or probability strikes you as an error; you shed it and fancy that this represents a victory for your reason. But perhaps this error was as necessary for you then, when you were still a different person . . . as are all your present "truths". . . . What killed that opinion for you was your new life and not your reason: *you no longer need it.* . . .[5]

How might we articulate the type of concern that Nietzsche raises in this passage? As I have already suggested, religious beliefs possess an existential aspect, which is another way of saying that they are connected in an important way to those commitments and projects that shape and in fact constitute a person's identity. Since Plantinga's analysis is limited to a discussion of the rational *permissibility* of religious beliefs, it fails to do justice to the complex ways these beliefs might be tied to those self-constitutive commitments that Charles Taylor calls "self-interpretations."[6] Once we expand our analysis to include the assessment not only of beliefs, but also those desires, interests, and intentions that are constitutive of the self, a whole host of new questions emerge.

Could it be the case, for example, that a person's loss of faith is not primarily a question of whether he or she ceases to believe in certain propositions? Might it not be the case that a loss of belief involves other deeper worries that surround changes and shifts in a person's basic concerns and commitments? Throughout this book I have explored some of the considerations that lead me to think that what is required is a more holistic way of speaking about this kind of assessment. In more Kierkegaardian terms, I have insisted that the ethics of belief is not a matter of assessing a person's religious convictions as isolated and objective propositions. It is rather a question of thinking about and assessing a person's "life-view" or "theory of life" as a whole.

In light of these brief and perhaps all too programmatic remarks it should be fairly clear that any attempt to do justice to the motivations behind a person's loss of faith must begin with a consideration of how such a loss is tied either to the erosion of a person's basic religious concerns or to attempts to restore commensurability in one's life by acknowledging the emergence of self-interpretations that conflict with one's religious views. Such an approach, I think, is quite different from those attempts to explicate the rationality of religious belief in terms of what is either obligatory or permissible for a person to believe. Plantinga's appeal to the notion of proper basicality is, it seems to me, a perfect example of this kind of rationalistic approach. As he insists, Christian beliefs are "inno-cent until proven guilty" and believers are within their "epistemic rights" to hold these beliefs even though no evidence can be given to sup-port them. Such a claim might serve as a good defeater against the argu-ments of someone such as John Locke or Anthony Flew, but it does not appear to do full justice to all the issues surrounding the ethics of belief.

If we want to understand the many ways a person's faith can be chal-lenged or lost, we must take a closer look at how religious beliefs are connected to those basic commitments, concerns, and emotions that constitute a person's character. In some instances, the challenge to some-one's faith might be less a question of whether the belief is rational in some minimal sense, and more a question of whether one's fundamental projects and concerns have been called into question. In this situation, the individual is confronted with a crisis of what could be called con-flicting self-interpretations, to borrow once again a phrase from Charles Taylor. When this happens, it is often hard to see how defeaters can ena-ble a person to sustain confidence in his religious convictions; for in cases such as these individuals who have been committed to the cultiva-tion of Christian self-understanding may realize that they can no longer make their lives intelligible in these terms. Furthermore, a failure or re-fusal to acknowledge a conflict of self-interpretations is not simply a failure of rationality or consistency. The failure runs much deeper and would be better described as a crisis of commensurability.[7] In cases such as these, what is required is not argument, but rather a willingness to acknowledge new possibilities for life and a desire to appropriate a more authentic understanding of oneself.

B. *Suffering, Evil, and the Loss of Faith*

One area of concern that highlights the implications of these con-siderations is the traditional theological debate concerning the problem of evil and the extent to which affliction and suffering can undermine a person's religious convictions. For the person who wants his or her relig-ious beliefs to reflect a faithful openness to reality, the dilemma is clear. On the one hand, we have seen that a person's religious beliefs are tied to those basic interests and concerns that are constitutive of the self. Since it is in terms of such basic interests and concerns that a person defends and articulates his or her other beliefs, such interests and concerns are not themselves open to justification.[8] In this respect, there is a grain of truth in Plantinga's analysis: one need not give reasons or evidence to support one's religious beliefs. Unlike Plantinga, however, I do not want to focus on the person's religious *beliefs* but rather on the entire ensemble of concerns, emotions, and interests that constitute one's life-view as a whole. What is properly basic then is not a set of beliefs but this life-view.

Even though we cannot make sense of the self-involving character of religious beliefs without some kind of appeal to commitment, the believer may still wonder whether such commitment has any limits. The problem of evil clearly raises this kind of question. The dilemma is whether it is possible to balance the kind of unconditional commitment that characterizes what Bernard Williams calls a person's "categorical desires"[9] with a willingness to acknowledge the possibility that the problem of evil might challenge and sometimes even undermine his or her religious beliefs.

Plantinga, of course, does not want to deny that the problem of evil is a potential defeater that the theist cannot simply ignore. However, although he appears to take such potential defeaters seriously, the Free Will Defense he offers as a response to the atheist's objections makes it difficult to see how a person could lose faith and invoke the existence of evil and suffering as a *reason* for this loss of faith. In *The Nature of Necessity*, as well as in his less technical discussion, *God, Freedom, and Evil*,[10] Plantinga gives a new twist to the traditional attempt to show that the existence of an omniscient, omnipotent, and benevolent God is consistent with the existence of evil. According to Plantinga, the theist need not attempt to formulate a theodicy that somehow explains the existence of evil. Such a strong defense is neither desirable nor required. His task is the more modest one of showing that God's existence, as traditionally understood, is *consistent* with the existence of evil.

Since my problems with Plantinga's solution to this issue have little to do with the details of his rather ingenious argument but more with general worries concerning the cogency of his approach, a brief sketch of his strategy will have to suffice. Plantinga wants to admit that an appeal to the proper basicality of religious beliefs is perfectly compatible with epistemic fallibilism. For this reason he takes seriously the possibility that the atheist's appeal to evil constitutes a prima facie defeater to theism. The solution, however, is not to provide a full-blown theodicy but rather to offer a defeater for the defeater. Such a defeater, argues Plantinga, is possible for the theist if he or she is willing to spell out the implications of several straightforward assumptions.

First, such a Free Will Defense will begin with the traditional claim that some good states of affairs might include, and in some instances actually entail, certain kinds of evil. I know it is a good thing for my dentist to fill my cavity but I also know that it is a very bad thing to drill at my all-too-tender nerves. Although the analogy is weak, the point is clear.

As Plantinga himself argues: "Certain kinds of values, certain good states of affairs, can't exist apart from evil of some sort."[11] Plantinga's claim is that one such good, which will *necessarily* involve the risk or possibility of evil, is moral good. For moral good is possible, argues Plantinga, only for those creatures that are significantly free. If, however, God creates people who are significantly free, he does so only at the risk of introducing the possibility of moral evil. The second crucial premise of Plantinga's argument is the claim that it might be possible that all such creatures who are significantly free suffer from "transworld depravity." In the final analysis, argues Plantinga, if we accept the claim that the possibility of moral good depends on the existence of creatures who are significantly free, and admit the existence of transworld depravity, then God simply could not have created a world containing moral good without the possibility that such a world might contain moral evil.

Plantinga realizes, of course, that his whole argument hinges on whether it is defensible to make such a claim; namely, that it "was not within God's power to create a world containing moral good without creating one containing moral evil."[12] By appealing to the notion of possible worlds, Plantinga believes that he can demonstrate in a rigorous manner that this claim is possible and that it is consistent with the claim that God is omnipotent, omniscient, and wholly good. Thus, by appealing to the resources of modal logic the theist can provide a defeater for the atheist's defeater and thus maintain, in an epistemically responsible way, his or her belief in God.

After working through Plantinga's Free Will Defense one cannot help but be impressed by the technical acumen and logical virtuosity of its author. Plantinga never sacrifices rigor or clarity in the presentation of his case and, despite the criticisms of J. L. Mackie and Anthony Kenny,[13] among others, has set forth a rather convincing argument. However, it is difficult not to be disappointed after working through this difficult argument if only because the outcome is rather thin. Perhaps one will agree with Plantinga that the existence of an omnipotent, omniscient, and benevolent God is *logically* consistent with the existence of evil. This would mean that it is permissible to maintain one's belief in God on the grounds that the Free Will Defense provides a prima facie defeater for the atheist's defeater. Unfortunately, such a defense is beside the point, especially for those people who view the problem of evil as a moral objection to theism. The question is whether an account of the ethics of belief needs to address why affliction and the problem of evil might lead such people to lose their faith.

Consider, for example, Ivan Karamazov's reflections on the problem of evil in Dostoyevski's *The Brothers Karamazov.* Two chapters before

Ivan delivers his famous speech on The Grand Inquisitor, he explains his views on religion to his brother Alyosha:

> And so I accept God and am glad to, and what's more I accept His wisdom, His purpose—which are utterly beyond our ken; I believe in the underlying order and the meaning of life; I believe in the eternal harmony in which they say we shall one day be blended. I believe in the Word to Which the universe is striving, and Which Itself was "with God," and Which Itself is God and so on, to infinity. There are all sorts of phrases for it. I seem to be on the right path, don't I? Yet would you believe it, in the final result I don't accept this world of God's, and, although I know it exists, I don't accept it at all. It's not that I don't accept God, you must understand, it's the world created by Him I don't and cannot accept.[14]

The point I want to emphasize here is that the subtlety of Ivan's observations highlights the inadequacies of an account such as the one offered by Plantinga. Plantinga himself, of course, maintains that Ivan's concerns are not really relevant to his concerns to the extent that they do not involve *philosophical* worries.[15] Presumably, Plantinga would want to argue that philosophical reflection is not really relevant here and what Ivan needs is some spiritual counseling. It seems to me, however, that such a way of construing Ivan's concerns is woefully misguided. There are some major issues of interest relevant to the ethics of belief debate which can be addressed only if we take Ivan's atheism seriously.[16] One might, for example, ask whether Ivan's objections to theism are legitimate or whether they are rooted in self-deception.[17] But in order to do justice to this type of question we need to consider a whole host of questions concerning those concerns that shape Ivan's self-understanding. Clearly, what needs to be assessed in this regard is not whether Ivan is or is not permitted to believe certain propositions. Very little here depends on what is or is not within Ivan's epistemic rights, whatever they might be. The lesson to be learned here is clear: in order to do justice to the ethics of belief we need to assess Ivan's entire life-view and this will entail a more detailed consideration of the way his religious convictions are bound up with his character as a whole.

I would like to insist then that if Ivan's atheism is in fact open to criticism, the case against him will need to account not only for the kind of argument he offers; it will need to consider the complex ways his argument is tied to his entire way of looking at things. Interestingly enough, Ivan himself, well aware that there is an important connection between his views about God and his character, suggests that this is a central consideration in our discussion about God and the meaning of life: "For what are we aiming at now? I am trying to explain as quickly as possible my essential nature, that is what manner of man I am, what I believe in, and for what I hope, that's it, isn't it?"[18] The inadequacy of Plantinga's Free Will Defense lies in its failure to illuminate the relevance of these kinds of considerations. Plantinga forecloses this kind of debate and constructive reflection about the problem of evil because he refuses to take seriously Ivan's important insight that we cannot discuss such fundamental questions without implicating our characters in an important way. As it turns out, when we take a closer look at the kind of person Ivan is, we realize that his arguments turn against him: Ivan indicts himself. Ironically though, Plantinga's account curtails argument at precisely that point where it might be most challenging to an atheist such as Ivan.

When we turn to consider Ivan's cynical and ruthless critique of Alyosha's theism it soon becomes clear that the shape of his argument is suspect and that there are good reasons to take him to task. What is perhaps most interesting to note about Ivan is that, like Plantinga, he manages to foreclose the possibility of debate. However, unlike Plantinga, who manages to foreclose substantive debate by an appeal to certain *logical* considerations, Ivan's avoidance of constructive debate is due to a flaw in his character. Even though it often appears as though Ivan has offered a convincing challenge to Alyosha's theism, the despair that grounds his negative views about God also blinds him to the possibility that there are other ways of thinking about God and the problem of suffering.

Although a detailed analysis of Book 5 of *The Brothers Karamazov* is beyond the scope of this volume, one of the things that we learn about Ivan is the degree to which his atheism depends on his ability to utilize subtle but complex strategies to evade the implications of his views. It is well known, for example, that what worries Ivan is the unredeemed suffering of the innocent, in particular, the suffering of innocent children. With respect to this question, Ivan quite rightly eschews the temptation to appeal to theodicies that appear to solve the problem by specious rationalizations:

> "I understand nothing," Ivan went on, as though in delirium. "I don't want to understand anything now. I want to stick to the fact. I made up my mind long ago not to understand. If I try to understand anything, I shall be false to the fact and I have determined to stick to the fact."[19]

Ivan is right to be suspicious of reductionism with respect to fundamental religious issues. For this reason he rejects any sort of speculative theodicy that presumes to justify or make sense of senseless suffering. One wonders, however, whether Ivan himself is guilty of his own subtle forms of reductionism that blinds him to other religious possibilities. Stewart Sutherland, for example, has suggested that Ivan's dilemma is due to the fact that he deliberately appeals to a false picture of God which may enable him to *legitimate* his religious rebellion.[20] According to Sutherland, it is no mere coincidence that Ivan's diatribe against theism and his famous Grand Inquisitor speech are delivered in the neighborhood pub. Sutherland's suggestion is that Ivan reduces God-talk to tavern-talk and thereby succeeds in trivializing the theist's claims. In this respect, Ivan's approach to the problem is no better than that of the theist who appeals to theodicies in order to secure his faith in an illegitimate fashion. One might even say that what Ivan offers Alyosha is an "antitheodicy" which is designed to protect him against anyone who might challenge his despair and rebellion. In the end, Ivan's atheism is secured by the same kind of reductionism for which he criticizes the theist who appeals to theodicies and other philosophical rationalizations to avoid any substantive challenge to his religious convictions.

C. Simone Weil and the Virtue of Attention

Strange as it seems Plantinga and Ivan Karamazov have each in their own way devised subtle and complex ways to avoid those difficult questions that might call their respective views into question. Of course, this should come as no surprise, especially when we remind ourselves that a person's beliefs about God or the meaning of life are tied to those self-interpretations that are constitutive of the self. To acknowledge the possibility that these basic self-constitutive commitments can be vulnerable is to acknowledge more serious possibilities of loss: loss of self and loss of one's world. For this reason, we are often tempted to refuse to acknowledge these possibilities and appeal instead to various strategies that could enable us to secure these basic concerns and commitments from anything that might threaten them. To borrow a phrase from the philosopher Harry Frankfurt, we care for our cares.[21] As we have already seen, this kind of concern for our cares is unavoidable for the simple reason that this characteristic of caring for one's cares is part of what it means to be a person. The question, however, is whether there are limits to these second-order cares and whether we should be more circumspect with respect to the strategies we use to guard and protect our basic concerns. For while commitment and loyalty to our basic cares and concerns are an essential part of our personhood, we cannot ignore the contingent and unpredictable claims of reality which might call these basic cares into question. But is it possible for a believer to care for his or her basic convictions and loyalties without appealing to strategies that would render them immune and invulnerable to those contingencies that call them into question? In short, is it possible to be a loyal believer while at the same time acknowledging the fragility of faith?

Simone Weil is one of the few religious thinkers who wants to call our attention to the many ways a person's religious beliefs can be challenged and put at risk and who is deeply concerned with how this possibility relates to the ethics of belief. Unlike those contemporary thinkers who still continue to spell out the dynamics of faith by appealing to the existentialist notion of commitment, Weil expresses serious misgivings about such volitionalist language and argues instead that our basic beliefs and concerns ought to conform to reality as it presents itself to us. For this reason, Weil eschews the traditional Kantian approach to knowledge which emphasizes the *activity* underlying all human understanding and emphasizes instead the *passivity* entailed by notions such as vision and attention. Although Weil would accept the suggestion that our cares and loyalties are often fragile and therefore require our loving attention, she clearly rejects the claim that a person's commitments constitute the final court of appeal. Because Weil values the idea of a truthful perception of the world, she rejects all strategies and philosophical ideologies that could lead to spiritual blindness.

When we turn to Weil's observations concerning these issues it soon becomes clear that her views are at odds both with those defended by Plantinga as well as with those presented by Ivan Karamazov. On the one hand, she is suspicious of the Christian who appeals to theodicies and other sophisticated philosophical rationalizations on the grounds that they blind us to evil and lead to a sense of ersatz security. In fact, Weil rejects not only theodicies but any kind of religious ideology or belief that blinds us to reality: "We must leave on one side the beliefs which fill up voids and sweeten what is bitter. The belief in immortality. The belief in the utility of sin: *etiam peccata*. The belief in the providential ordering of events—in short the 'consolations' which are ordinarily sought in religion."[22] The point is, of course, that she clearly shares Ivan's suspicion of any explanation that suggests that there might be a reason for the suffering of innocent people. Weil, like Ivan, would categorically reject theodicies or other strategies which might remove the difficulty of being a Christian.

However, it is important to remember that while Weil shares Ivan's suspicion of theodicies, she would be highly critical of his own antitheodicy to the extent that such an antitheodicy merely expresses his own sense of blind defiance and outrage. As a person who believes in God, Weil leaves no doubt regarding her views on this matter. In her book

Gravity and Grace her brief observations concerning Ivan highlight the similarities as well as the differences between their views:

> Speech of Ivan in the *Karamazovs*: 'Even though his immense factory were to produce the most extraordinary marvels and were to cost only a single tear from a single child, I refuse.'
>
> I am in complete agreement with this sentiment. No reason whatever which anyone could produce to compensate for a child's tear. Absolutely none which the mind can conceive. There is just one, however, but it is intelligible only to supernatural love: 'God willed it'. And for that reason I would consent to a world which was nothing but evil as readily to a child's tear.[23]

At first glance Weil's remark might come as some surprise, especially since she explicitly condones Ivan's rejection of theodicy while appearing to offer her own theistic rationalization of human suffering. What are we to make of this apparent contradiction? Although this passage might appear to pose some difficult problems, we must not forget that Weil is offering neither a theodicy nor a subtle strategy to avoid the problem. In fact, when Weil invokes the phrase 'God willed it' to articulate her difference from Ivan, we must remember that such a remark is *not* intended to serve as an *explanation* that helps reconcile belief in God with the problem of human suffering. On the contrary, Weil's observation here is best understood as a grammatical remark, to borrow a phrase from Wittgenstein, and serves precisely to remind us of the limits of explanation. The phrase 'God willed it' gives us no new information about the world and serves as a kind of shorthand to remind us where certain kinds of religious assertions come to an end.

Some, of course, might object to my characterization of Weil's view and insist that her position is no less objectionable than that of the naive theist whom Ivan criticizes. Although an objection such as this might appear to have some merit, it fails to take seriously my basic thesis that the ethics of belief is *not* simply a question of assessing the rational acceptability of a person's particular beliefs. What we need to consider instead is the way a person's religious beliefs are tied to his or her character as a whole. The real difference, therefore, between Weil and the naive theist will need to be articulated in terms of their respective responses to suffering and evil. As Kierkegaard reminds us, the question is a subjective one which centers not so much on *what* a person believes but rather on *how* a person believes. Does the theist appeal to rationalizations to minimize or evade the difficulties that pose a challenge to his or her beliefs? If so, then it might make sense to suggest that such a person is blameworthy. If we examine Weil's religious writings, however, it is clear that she refuses to trivialize the problem of evil in this way and acknowledges repeatedly the extent to which suffering and affliction can render one's religious beliefs vulnerable. In short, Weil acknowledges the fragility of faith.

With respect to the problem of evil then it might be helpful to spell out the ethics of belief in terms of the language of virtues and vices. On the one hand, Weil, like Ivan, warns us against those theodicies and philosophical rationalizations that lead to a kind of pernicious complacency and the vice of blindness. By the same token, it is also clear that Weil wants to reject the vice of defiance that underlies Ivan's rejection of God. As Sutherland points out in his discussion of atheism, it is this kind of consideration that distinguishes the views of Simone Weil from those of someone such as Albert Camus who wants to condone Ivan's rebellion as a heroic act. As Sutherland rightly notes, Weil would probably characterize Ivan's atheism not as an expression of heroic rebellion, but rather as a vice: the vice of blind self-assertion.[24]

What then is the virtue to which we can appeal as the proper mean between the vice of blindness and the vice of defiance? According to Weil, the appropriate response to the problem of evil is neither the rationalistic appeal to theodicy nor is it the act of blind rebellion: it is rather the act of waiting (*attente*) and consent: "The attitude which brings about salvation is not like any form of activity. The Greek word which expresses it is *hypomene*, and *patientia* is rather an inadequate translation of it."[25]

Although Weil herself never makes explicit mention of the ethics of belief, her writings are filled with observations that give us a good clue regarding her views on this subject. As already mentioned, Weil wants to call our attention to the many ways seeking a solution to the problem of evil distorts the true perception of reality. "Seeking," she says, "leads us astray. This is the case with every form of what is truly good. Man should do nothing but wait for the good and keep evil away."[26] Weil believes that it is impossible for a person to accept affliction willingly: the most we can do is to consent to evil with the hope that it might yield a truer perception of things.

What is important to remember with respect to Weil's appeal to consent is that it is a response that allows us to make sense of the fragility of faith. Unlike many Christian thinkers and philosophers, Weil is willing to acknowledge that evil and suffering can make it impossible for a Christian to love God and is even willing to grant that evil and affliction could lead to a loss of faith:

It is when I am in contact with the affliction of other people, those who are indifferent or unknown to me as much as the others, perhaps even more, including those of the most remote ages of antiquity. This contact causes me such atrocious pain and so utterly rends my soul, that as a result the love of God becomes almost impossible for me for a while. It would take very little more to make me say impossible.[27]

What makes Weil's observation so important is that she is willing to acknowledge the possibility that evil and suffering might make it impossible for a person to love God. Unlike Ivan Karamazov who appears to appeal to the suffering of innocent people to legitimate his outrage and rebellion, Weil accepts God and His world. Whereas Ivan responds with contempt, Weil responds with love. On the other hand, Weil differs from Plantinga in that she is aware that faith in the face of evil is a fragile thing which cannot be preserved by an act of will or by ignoring the problem. In the end, faith is a vulnerable gift which the believer must submit to the care of grace.

Notes

1. Simone Weil, "Human Personality" in *The Simone Weil Reader*, ed. George A. Panichas (New York: David McKay Company, 1977), p. 332.

2. This turn of phrase is intended as a reminder that this book is in keeping with the spirit of Martha Nussbaum's *The Fragility of Goodness: Luck and Ethics in Greek Tragedy and Philosophy* (Cambridge: Cambridge University Press, 1986).

3. Alvin Plantinga, "Reason and Belief in God," in *Faith and Rationality: Reason and Belief in God* (Notre Dame: University of Notre Dame Press, 1983), pp. 16–93.

4. For a more detailed treatment of what can constitute a "defeater" as well as a "defeater of a defeater" see Richard Foley, *The Epistemic Theory of Rationality* (Cambridge: Harvard University Press, 1987), pp. 18ff. The distinction between potential and genuine defeaters is treated on pp. 42ff.

5. Friedrich Nietzsche, *The Gay Science*, trans. Walter Kaufmann (New York: Viking Press, 1974), pp. 245–46.

6. Charles Taylor, "Self-Interpreting Animals," in *Human Agency and Language: Philosophical Papers I* (London: Cambridge University Press, 1985), pp. 45–76.

7. The dynamics that underlie this kind of scenario are explored by Thomas S. Kuhn in his well-known book *The Structure of Scientific Revolutions* (Chicago: University of Chicago Press, 1970).

8. Bernard Williams, *Moral Luck: Philosophical Papers 1973–1980* (Cambridge: Cambridge University Press, 1981), pp. 1–19.

9. Ibid.

10. Alvin Plantinga, *The Nature of Necessity* (Oxford: Clarendon Press, 1974) and *God, Freedom, and Evil* (Grand Rapids: William B. Eerdman, 1977).

11. Plantinga, *God, Freedom, and Evil*, p. 23.

12. Ibid., p. 54.

13. See J. L. Mackie, *The Miracle of Theism* (Oxford: Clarendon Press, 1982), esp. pp. 173–76, and Anthony Kenny, *The God of the Philosophers* (Oxford: Clarendon Press, 1979), esp. p. 70.

14. Fyodor Dostoyevski, *The Brothers Karamazov*, trans. Constance Garnett, rev. and ed. Ralph E. Matlaw (New York: W. W. Norton, 1976), p. 216.

15. Plantinga, *God, Freedom, and Evil*, pp. 63–64.

16. A good example of how Ivan's atheism lends itself to philosophical reflection can be found in Stewart Sutherland's *Atheism and the Rejection of God* (Oxford: Basil Blackwell, 1977), esp. pp. 25–40.

17. As we shall see, it is a gross oversimplification to interpret Ivan's rebellion as an act of heroic defiance in the face of God's cosmic cruelty and injustice. For all its flourish, Ivan's convincing rhetoric is rooted in self-deception. In his critical biography of Dostoyevski, the scholar and critic Konstantin Mochulsky sums up this view when he states: "the keenness of Ivan's reasoning lies in that he renounces God *out of love for mankind*, comes forward against the Creator in the role of the advocate of all suffering creation. In this imposture is hidden a diabolic deceit." See Konstantin Mochulsky, *Dostoevsky: His Life and Work*, trans. Michael A. Minihan (Princeton: Princeton University Press, 1971), p. 616.

18. Dostoyevski, *The Brothers Karamazov*, p. 216.

19. Ibid., p. 224.

20. Sutherland sums up his views quite nicely in the following observation: "Ivan sets about trivializing religious belief, by suggesting that the language of religion has as its appropriate home, idle chatter.

The role which it can meaningfully play in the life of men is at best that of diversion, more probably that of adding to the flow of the garrulous. Now, there is no doubt that it can play this latter role! The question is, Can it play any other?" *Atheism and the Rejection of God*, p. 39.

21. Harry Frankfurt, *The Importance of What We Care About: Philosophical Essays* (Cambridge: Cambridge University Press, 1988).

22. Simone Weil, *Gravity and Grace*, trans. Emma Craufurd (London: Ark Paperbacks, 1987).

23. Ibid., p. 68.

24. Sutherland notes: "Camus sees the anger and outrage of rebellion as of potentially fundamental value in coming to terms with the world in which we live, while at the same time, in Ivan's words 'sticking to the facts'. Simone Weil sees this form of anger and outrage as ultimately destructive of love and compassion." *Atheism and the Rejection of God*, p. 67.

25. Simone Weil, *Waiting for God*, trans. Emma Craufurd (London: Routledge and Kegan Paul, 1979), p. 128.

26. Ibid.

27. Ibid., p. 39.

7

Reductionism and the Ethics of Belief

"Faith" is a fine invention
When Gentlemen can *see*
But Microscopes are prudent
In an Emergency.
Emily Dickinson[1]

A. *Worrying about Reduction*

The best way to articulate the problem of reductionism in the study of religion is to speak of the ever-present temptation to overcome the strange and alien by means of what I like to call "hermeneutical domestication." Disagreement and misunderstanding are, of course, facts of life and it is perhaps natural at times to think that disagreement might be a threat to our sense of rationality. Our suspicion is that when we disagree—about morality, religion, or politics—there must either be a way to overcome the problem, to discover the elusive third term that might reveal that we never really did disagree in the first place, *or*, when disagreement seems intractable, to hope that there is some way to *explain* it away. Troubled by the prospect that there could be a strange and alien tribe with customs, beliefs, and practices quite different from ours, we struggle to overcome the strangeness by redescribing what their tribe does in terms that are familiar. When all-out war seems impracticable, we seek to conquer by other means. The safest alternative is usually some form of reductionism.

It is important to remember, of course, that the specter of reductionism presents itself as an unavoidable temptation whenever we seek to understand a new and strange phenomenon. Our first response as we struggle to come to terms with the unfamiliar is to appeal to familiar categories and concepts that we already possess in order to make sense of our experience. After all, when we begin our investigation, these are the only resources at our disposal. In this sense, reduction is an unavoidable and acceptable first step in coming to terms with the world.

Problems arise, however, when this initial strategy to seek understanding becomes a means of evading the hermeneutical anxiety that results when we sense that the unfamiliar has called *our* way of making sense of the world into question. When this happens, our uneasiness can lead to a wide variety of strategies to cope with this anxiety. More often than not, we are tempted to alleviate this uneasiness by struggling to regain control of the situation. Not only do we refuse to acknowledge important differences, we resort to radical redescriptions of beliefs and practices that distort them. In seeking to secure epistemic control in this obsessive fashion, we risk losing access to reality. The risk of reductionism in this bad sense leads to a loss of objectivity.

Unfortunately, many contemporary philosophers, anthropologists, and students of religion fail to see exactly why reductionism is a problem for the simple reason that they do not view it as a problem of the *ethics* of belief. For the most part, reductionism tends to be treated as an epistemological problem under the rubric of rationality or relativism. The hope of many philosophers is that a careful and detailed account of rationality or a critique of relativism along the lines proposed by Donald Davidson[2] will enable us to deal with and finally dissolve many of the important worries surrounding this issue.

On the side of the so-called relativists, thinkers such as D. Z. Phillips and Peter Winch are terribly concerned about the tendency of some people to distort the meaning of religious beliefs by explaining them away and hope that an appeal to the work of Wittgenstein will provide the resources for a critique of reductionism. More recently, the worries that Phillips and Winch express about reductionism have been challenged by people such as Wayne Proudfoot, who argues that these thinkers overstate their case against reductionism and that the explanatory reductionism required by the social scientific study of religion is perfectly legitimate.

In the course of this chapter I will suggest that although Phillips, Winch, and Proudfoot have all raised important questions and issues for those interested in the study of religion, the terms of the debate need to be expanded to show why reductionism is a genuine concern for anyone interested in the ethics of belief. On the one hand, although Phillips's concerns about the relationship between explanation and religious belief are based on legitimate worries, his alternative to reductionism entails an unacceptable form of naive relativism. Such a response to the problem of reductionism does away with the disagreement between the believer and the unbeliever by suggesting that a scientific account of religious belief distorts its true character and that the believer and the unbeliever are simply not talking about the same thing. Proudfoot, on the other hand, while rightly acknowledging that all forms of explanation depend on some kind of reductionism, fails to acknowledge the many ways explanation can serve as a strategy for domesticating strange and unfamilar beliefs we may not share. Like Phillips, Proudfoot wants to overcome the hermeneutical anxiety occasioned by our disagreements and does so by appealing to explanation. For Proudfoot, however, the unfamiliarity of strange and alien beliefs is overcome to the extent that we have explained them in terms familiar to us.

Throughout this chapter it should become clear that I am suspicious of any attempt to rationalize our disagreements by appealing to any philosophical account that might ease the perplexity often occasioned by such differences. Unlike those who hope that worries about reductionism can be put to rest by a clarification of the epistemological issues at stake, I believe that the problem of what I call radical disagreement requires another approach. Once again, I am tempted to invoke the language of Stanley Cavell who suggests throughout his writings that it is a mistake to offer philosophical theories to explain our failures to understand each other. On the contrary, our failures to understand each other are tied to our failures and refusals to acknowledge what others hold to be important.

Reductionism is an issue worthy of our attention to the extent that it can be understood as one way of articulating the need to cope with such failures of acknowledgment. The feeling that we can no longer make sense of another's beliefs, desires, or emotions is often the cause of bewilderment—what I have already called hermeneutical anxiety. When this happens, the fear is that the world no longer makes sense, an apprehension which in turn can lead to the erosion of our confidence in our way of looking at things. The temptation then is to regain control by a process of hermeneutical domestication—to render the strange, the unknown, the alien, harmless by means of conceptual redescription. Reductionism becomes a rather problematic way of coping with our finitude, a strategy that enables us to come to terms with our failures of understanding. It is in some sense the human-all-too-human response to our desire to ensure and secure confidence in our rationality.

B. The Case against Reduction

Writers such as D. Z. Phillips and Peter Winch appropriate Wittgenstein's enigmatic remarks concerning "forms of life" and "language games" in order to criticize what they regard as reductionistic distortions of religion and ritual. In his well-known book *Religion Without Explanation*,[3] for example, Phillips challenges a whole host of theories that purport to *explain* religion in nonreligious terms. Anthropologists, sociologists, psychologists, and many philosophers are guilty, says Phillips, of a kind of theoretical myopia that blinds them to the genuine meaning of religious language and practice. Although his criticisms of these theories vary, depending on the specific point of contention, it is possible to identify a general worry that informs the entire work. More specifically, Phillips, like Wittgenstein, is wary of the kind of "scientism" which often underlies the analysis of religion offered by its many secular critics. According to Phillips, the tendency to *explain* religion is motivated by the common but mistaken assumption that there is only one legitimate form of rationality; namely, scientific rationality. As Phillips argues throughout his book, such an assumption is fundamentally misguided and leads to a distorted view of religious beliefs and practices.

Phillips's critique of the many classical theories that claim to offer plausible and defensible explanations of religion begins with a critical but basically sympathetic appraisal of David Hume's contribution to the philosophy of religion. First of all, Phillips seems to accept the validity of Hume's compelling objections to natural theology and other kinds of rationalistic attempts to justify religious beliefs. But this sympathetic reading of Hume should not come as any surprise, given Phillips's Wittgensteinian assumption that it is a mistake to ask for any such justification in the first place.

The main concern underlying Phillips's treatment of Hume, however, is what he takes to be the mistaken view of those who believe that the rejection of natural theology necessarily entails the indefensibility of religion. The problem is that once people begin to suspect that religious beliefs cannot be justified, they jump to the conclusion that such beliefs must either be confused or false. But once we suspect that a person's religious beliefs are false, we are tempted to search for some explanation that might account for why a false or confused belief should be accepted by so many people. Phillips insists, however, that this line of reasoning is itself radically confused and is based on a distorted picture of religious life. In the end then Phillips appeals to the work of Wittgenstein to show that there is a more acceptable way to characterize religious belief that escapes both Hume's valid objections to natural theology as well as the reductionistic explanations of religion offered by his many successors.

Because I am primarily interested in the issue of reductionism and not in the wide variety of explanatory theories explored by Phillips, I will not examine the theories themselves, nor will I assess the validity of his detailed criticisms. What interests me, rather, are the reasons why he sus-

pects that any attempt to understand religious beliefs and practices in social scientific terms is somehow illicit. There are, of course, many different ways to characterize reductionism as well as a wide variety of reasons
to reject it as an objectionable strategy of understanding. Sometimes, for
example, Phillips suggests that the most dangerous assumption underlying reductionistic approaches to religion is the mistaken belief that the
only valid form of rationality is scientific rationality. Appealing to the
writings of Cook Wilson, Phillips challenges the powerful but often un-
acknowledged dogma that any belief, practice, or activity that does not
conform to this standard is either false or confused. The problem, concludes Phillips, is that if we adhere to such a monolithic standard to determine the value of our beliefs and practices, there is much we would be
forced to ignore or discount as unintelligible. The writings of Wilson, argues Phillips, suggest another, more acceptable alternative:

> His point could be expressed more clearly if we said that
> through an investigation of various human activities associated
> with science, religion, morality, art, politics, etc., one may be
> brought to see that there is no one paradigm of rationality to
> which all human activity has to conform.[4]

In addition to Phillips's concern that reductionism rests on an inde-
fensibly narrow view of rationality is a second and closely related objection. In his critical analysis of the work of E. B. Tylor and James Frazer,
for example, Phillips notes that more often than not reductionism is
motivated by the zeal of so-called enlightened reformers who view the
scientific explanation as a remedy for ignorance and superstition. Phillips himself, for instance, characterizes Tylor's project in the following
terms: "In giving an account of the kind of beliefs magical and religious
beliefs are, and revealing the mistakes involved in them, Tylor's enquiry
had a missionary zeal. He wanted to lead men from error to the truth, out
of darkness into light."[5] Clearly, Phillips has identified one of the central concerns that have informed critiques of religion since the Enlightenment, from Spinoza's *A Theologico-Political Treatise*, to Hume's
The Natural History of Religion. Indeed, few would deny that the work
of those nineteenth-century anthropologists cited by Phillips is motivated by the kind of agnostic and atheistic scrupulosity we tend to associate with the Victorian conscience. Nor is there any reason to take
Phillips to task when he reiterates his concern with reference to the
work of Sigmund Freud, who not only believes that it is possible to explain
religion in psychoanalytic terms, but hopes that a scientific understanding of religion might eventually lead to our psychic liberation. In most
cases then explanations of religion have not simply been undertaken in
the neutral and disinterested spirit of scientific research. On the contrary,

Phillips suspects that most reductionistic accounts of religion are motivated by a tacit ideological suspicion that all religious belief and practice is superstitious and therefore pernicious. In short, such explanations are often intended as "cures" for an allegedly pathological way of living.

The fact that reductionistic accounts of religion tend to foster a certain suspicion of religion leads Phillips to identify a third objection to reductionism. The problem with such accounts, suggests Phillips, is that they tend to blind us to other plausible ways of interpreting religious beliefs and rituals. For example, if one accepts the conclusions of Tylor or Frazer, who argue that religious beliefs and practices reflect mistaken scientific theories or hypotheses, one might fail to appreciate the *expressive* dimension of such activities. Given the "scientific" framework of the Victorian anthropologist, the only way to understand the gestures of those people who wave at a sunrise is to suppose that such activities are intended by them as a superstitious attempt to *cause* the sunrise. But why not follow Wittgenstein's suggestion, asks Phillips, and interpret the gesture as a greeting? This is not to say, of course, that Phillips's expressivist interpretation of ritual is either the most plausible or acceptable account in every case. The point, rather, is that such an approach can help us gain some critical leverage on other proposals which tend to rule out a priori other viable possibilities for interpretation.

Phillips develops this kind of objection to reductionism in more detail when he turns to consider the account of religion offered by Freud. According to Phillips, Freud's basic error stems from a mistaken view that religious beliefs are basically symptoms of neurosis. This basic misunderstanding leads Freud to distort the meaning of a person's religious beliefs by identifying them under descriptions that this particular person may not accept. Once again, the problem with this kind of approach, suggests Phillips, is that it leads to a kind of myopia: a refusal to take seriously the possibility that certain kinds of explanations blind us to the richness of a particular form of life.

What is particularly disturbing about Freud's account, insists Phillips, is his tendency to engage in fallacious generalizations and to employ psychoanalytic categories, which might be valid and even provide insight in individual cases, to assess practices, rituals, and religious institutions as a whole. This type of strategy, says Phillips, occurs over and over again throughout Freud's writings on religion and is indicative of the basic category mistake that vitiates many of his views concerning religion. Phillips expresses this particular objection in very clear and convincing terms:

> The point which needs to be emphasized is that social institutions, movements, and traditions cannot be explained in terms

of neurosis, since it is within the context of such institutions, movements, and traditions that neurosis has its meaning. When Freud speaks of the whole of primitive religion as a neurosis, he is employing an unhistorical notion of neurosis which is devoid of meaning.[6]

The upshot of the critique offered by Phillips is that Freud's tendency to treat religion as a neurosis tends to result in a variety of confusions. Once again, this is not to deny that in *some* situations a person's religious beliefs might be implicated in his or her particular neurosis. But this is a contingent matter that depends on the specific features of the case in question and *not* on the nature of religious belief. That is to say, even though Freud may be right to suggest that there are cases where one's religious beliefs could figure in the explanation of one's neurosis, this does *not* entail the stronger and implausible generalization that neurosis might help to explain religious belief. The problem is that once we succumb to this kind of illusion, we fail to see the subtle and complex ways a person's religious beliefs are in fact tied to the shape of his emotional and psychic life as a whole.

Another writer who challenges the reductionistic character of the social sciences along Wittgensteinian lines is Peter Winch. In his well-known monograph, *The Idea of a Social Science*,[7] for example, Winch critically examines the work of social scientists who fail to appreciate the many ways the criteria for the intelligibility of religious beliefs are tied to specific forms of life. Like Phillips, Winch draws on the insights of the later Wittgenstein and maintains that many anthropologists and sociologists unwittingly distort the meaning of a society's beliefs and rituals by importing their own standards of rationality in order to understand and evaluate foreign ways of life. Not surprisingly then Winch's discussion, like the position of D. Z. Phillips, has become a trademark of the view commonly known as Wittgensteinian fideism as well as the standard foil for more recent and sophisticated criticisms of relativism. In large part, most of these criticisms are well founded. But by the same token, even though it is impossible to deny the validity of the critical responses that comprise what is now the voluminous literature generated by Winch's writings, many of his important insights tend to be overlooked.

In order to gain a better idea of the general concerns raised by Winch throughout his work, it may be helpful to examine briefly his essay "Understanding a Primitive Society," written after *The Idea of a Social Science* in response to the criticisms of Alasdair MacIntyre. Winch begins by considering the work of E. E. Evans-Pritchard and suggests that even though he agrees with this anthropologist on many points, there are some important points of contention. More specifically, Winch is concerned about the uncritical way that Evans-Pritchard appeals to the notion of "objective reality" in order to legitimate his own scientific assessment of foreign cultures such as the Azande. The problem, says Winch, is that even though Evans-Pritchard is usually sensitive to the differences of radically different ways of life, he mistakenly assumes that his own scientific criteria of rationality grant him some privileged access to "objective reality" and that this standard entitles him to reject competing views as false. Unfortunately, continues Winch, this sort of view is based on the confused idea that scientific inquiry provides us with an independent check on reality not afforded by other ways of thinking about the world. The question, however, is whether it is possible to make sense of this way of talking.

Winch himself suspects that Evans-Pritchard is mistaken precisely to the extent that he is held captive to the confused picture that reality is independent of language. Winch characterizes what he considers to be the correct picture in the following terms:

> Reality is not what gives language sense. What is real and what is unreal shows itself *in* the sense that language has. Further, both the distinction between the real and the unreal and the concept of agreement with reality themselves belong to our language.[8]

According to Winch, therefore, Evans-Pritchard's desire to say that our beliefs and practices are correct when assessed with respect to some "objective" standard of reality is based on a misguided view of the relationship between language and the world. What Winch appears to be saying is that there is no way to compare the beliefs of the Azande and the scientific views of the twentieth-century anthropologist. To use the jargon that has become fashionable in some philosophical circles, these so-called "language games" are incommensurable to the extent that there is no independent neutral framework in terms of which a comparison can be made. In the end it is claims such as this that justify our sense that Winch's position deserves the dubious distinction of being labeled relativist.

Responses to the views of people such as Phillips and Winch are legion and any attempt to consider in detail the wide range of criticisms would take us too far afield. Initial responses, drawn, for example, from critics such as Alasdair MacIntyre, raise worries about whether it is possible for the relativist to account for the possibility of understanding.[9] On the face of it, an account such as that offered by Winch, who denies that we can evaluate by our standards the beliefs and practices of another culture, makes it difficult to see how we can even begin the difficult task of interpretation. Similar arguments against relativism have been offered by Donald Davidson whose classic article "On the Very Idea of a Conceptual Scheme"[10] presents a more sophisticated and nuanced treatment of the kinds of concerns that motivate MacIntyre's discussion. In light of such devastating criticisms one might suspect that there is little to recommend the views of someone such as Winch or Phillips.

Although the standard criticisms of relativism are well founded, there still might be a grain of truth that motivates the writings of Wittgensteinians such as Phillips and Winch. The problem is that both Phillips and Winch voice legitimate concerns that are often overlooked because the debate surrounding reductionism is, for the most part, misleadingly cast in terms of such issues as rationality and relativism. When we reconsider the work of Wittgenstein himself, however, it will become clear that the most defensible and forceful objections to reductionism are ethical ones, in the broad sense of that term. So even though there might be good Davidsonian grounds for rejecting the kind of relativism we find in the work of Phillips or Winch, there still might be good reasons to share their suspicion of reductionism.

C. The Case for Explanatory Reduction

Before we turn to consider this alternative way of articulating and defending these more plausible objections to reductionism, however, we need to consider the original and insightful defense of explanatory reduction recently offered by Wayne Proudfoot in his study *Religious Experience*.[11] Unlike many philosophers and social scientists who tend to concentrate on the problem of reductionism in isolation from their positive views on the nature of religion, Proudfoot situates his discussion of reductionism in the context of more general questions about human experience and religious studies. In other words, Proudfoot's defense of reductionism is a necessary prolegomena to his more general claim that it is perfectly legitimate to explain religious experience in naturalistic terms and that cognitive psychology and attribution theory might provide important resources for this kind of project.

For the most part, Proudfoot's analysis turns on the suggestion that the debate concerning reductionism has traditionally been cast in misleading terms. On the one hand, Proudfoot grants that there is something to be said for those critics of reductionism who rightly insist that the beliefs, actions, and experiences of a person must be identified under descriptions intelligible to the person in question. Drawing, in part, upon the work of Elizabeth Anscombe and others, Proudfoot agrees that there is something wrong in the strategy of the descriptive reductionist who redescribes a person's experience in such a way as to mischaracterize it. It would be a mistake, for example, to suppose that Socrates was afraid that the people of Athens might perish in a nuclear war. There are many ways of characterizing the possible fears of an ancient philosopher: plagues, droughts, and famines are just a few of the more plausible candidates. It would be a mistake, however, to appeal to the concept of nuclear war because such a description of Socrates' experience would be blatantly anachronistic.

Proudfoot, however, is well aware that the task of understanding the beliefs, actions, and experiences of others requires much more than the kind of grammatical elucidation necessary for characterizing an experience under the appropriate description. After all, once the social scientist has fixed the description of an experience or a practice in the appropriate terms, there is no reason why he or she should refrain proposing a hypothesis or theory to account for the data. For this reason, Proudfoot insists that it is not only legitimate, but necessary, to draw a subtle distinction between what he calls descriptive and explanatory reductionism.

As already mentioned, Proudfoot would agree that descriptive reductionism is illicit since it distorts the experience in question. Because the social scientist wants to explain why an individual or community characterizes their experience in the specific terms that they do, descriptive reductionism would be ruled out for the simple reason that it distorts the evidence. However, once the *explanandum* has been fixed by engaging in what Clifford Geertz has termed "thick description," Proudfoot believes that the scientist is free to engage in explanatory reductionism and to offer an *explanans* or hypothesis. And what is perhaps most important to remember about explanatory reductionism, says Proudfoot, is that once we have completed the descriptive task, a scientist is perfectly free to appeal to his or her own explanatory categories. In other words, unlike description, where our interpretation is necessarily constrained by the conceptual repertoire acknowledged by the individual or community in question, explanation *need not be restricted to terms acceptable to the person or culture we want to understand.*

We should not be surprised then if critics of reductionism express some misgivings concerning Proudfoot's analysis and his defense of explanatory reductionism as a perfectly valid and legitimate strategy for the social scientist. However, before we raise some critical questions regarding his position, we must remind ourselves that his recommendations concerning the study of religion make explicit some important and undeniable assumptions about the dynamics of human understanding. First of all, Proudfoot's analysis makes sense of our ordinary intuitions concerning interpretation and explanation and does justice to our wellfounded suspicion that "reductionism," in some form or another, is an unavoidable part of understanding. As I suggested above, when we attempt to make sense of a strange and alien way of life, we are forced at some point to draw on our own conceptual resources. It is futile to pretend that the issues, problems, and questions that we bring to our investigation have not been shaped by the bias of our own particular culture and training. In this respect, the various explorations of religion offered by Friedrich Nietzsche, Emile Durkheim, and Max Weber, to name just a few, deserve our serious attention. Even if we grant that theories offered by these thinkers are informed and motivated by tacit concerns and commitments that sometimes distort the data, it is a mistake to dismiss them in the way that Phillips often does in his critique. On the contrary, what is required is an appreciation of the way such explanatory strategies provide opportunities for discovery of something new about the importance of religion in human life. Unfortunately, Phillips and Winch are so concerned about the way social scientific approaches sometimes blind us to new possibilities of understanding, that they forget how often such investigation can open the way for new and fruitful interpretations of religious experience. In short, antireductionists, such as Phillips and Winch, who argue that certain approaches to religion are inherently confused, can be taken to task for their own more subtle form of reductionism to the extent that they seem to reject in an a priori fashion certain kinds of questions about human life.

Proudfoot's account suggests that there is no good reason for us to reject social scientific approaches to religion or to rule out the validity of explanatory theories, as long as proper care has been taken to describe the experience in the appropriate terms. For in our attempts to make sense of beliefs, practices, and experiences we may not share, we may find it necessary to formulate some hypothesis or theory, even though this theory is framed in terms neither acceptable nor intelligible to the people in question. Thus, the challenge is not to ignore the presuppositions that motivate and inform our quest for understanding but rather to develop a critical self-consciousness concerning the benefits and liabilities inherent in our particular point of view. Although there is no algorithm to ensure that we have reached an adequate understanding of a particular person, community, or culture, Proudfoot's distinction between descriptive and explanatory reduction provides a helpful heuristic device for the social scientific study of religion.

In spite of the merits of Proudfoot's proposal, several important questions must be addressed if we hope to clarify the difficult issue of reduction and religion. One particularly vexing problem centers on the reasons that motivate Proudfoot to draw this distinction between the two forms of reductionism in the first place. As already mentioned, if we view the distinction as a heuristic device for clarifying the complex process of investigation, it can be very helpful. Unfortunately, however, Proudfoot is not as clear on this point as we would hope. Sometimes, for example, his analysis seems to suggest that it is desirable to invoke and defend a distinction between descriptive and explanatory reduction because such a distinction seems to secure a privileged place for the social scientific approach over and against, say, a hermeneutical approach. One gets the impression, moreover, that the explanation of a person's experience is not only different from a description of it, but that an explanation is "authoritative" in a way that the description is not. One could almost say that although the description of a person's experience must be characterized in terms he would accept, the appeal to the notion of explanatory reduction appears to authorize a presumption in favor of the investigator's social scientific account of the experience.

In order to clarify my misgivings about the distinction, let me begin by calling attention to the simple and perhaps trivial fact that what Proudfoot calls explanatory reduction generally becomes an issue only for those who are already convinced that the subject's description entails or includes claims that we cannot accept. One way to bring out the significance of this observation is to consider the conversion story of Stephen Bradley cited by William James in his *Varieties of Religious Experience*. According to Proudfoot, who offers his own analysis of this episode in his book, the descriptive reductionist who fails to characterize Bradley's experience in religious terms has distorted it. What is needed, says Proudfoot, is an accurate characterization of Bradley's experience in terms he would accept. Proudfoot points out, however, that it is perfectly legitimate to *explain* Bradley's experience in terms he may not accept and seems to suggest that this move is authorized by a distinction between two different kinds of reductionism. In this instance, for example, one might appeal to the James-Lange theory of emotion or to Stanley Schachter's "attribution theory" as two possible and plausible explanations of his conversion. Indeed, Bradley is not likely to accept the account offered by the attribution theorist; but then again, there is no reason to expect this nor, as Proudfoot reminds us, should this trouble us. In the end, however, Proudfoot insists that such a move is perfectly legitimate and justified in light of what he says concerning the distinction between descriptive and explanatory reduction.

I wonder, however, whether the appeal to this kind of distinction is a misleading way of characterizing and defending someone's straightforward and justifiable interest in *explaining* rather than just *describing* Bradley's conversion. One might begin, for example, by asking *why* anyone would want to ask for a *further* explanation of Bradley's experience in the first place. After all, Bradley himself seems to offer a complete and coherent account. He openly confesses that his conversion is an expression of a divine purpose and characterizes his experience as the work of the Holy Spirit. What more is needed? If one happens to believe in God and the Holy Spirit, nothing more is required. Bradley's conversion account would be a source of perplexity only for the person who has good grounds to suspect (1) either that this particular event is not in fact the work of the Holy Spirit or (2) that the Holy Spirit does not exist. This is not to deny, of course, that Bradley believes his account is true and that we must characterize the experience in terms acceptable to him if we want to explain it. But this is precisely the point: a person would have no need to *explain* why Bradley characterizes his experience as the work of the Holy Spirit unless he had good grounds to think that *this* is really *not* the case. And since *what* I want to understand is why Bradley believes the particular things he says about his experience, I would be defeating the purpose of asking the question if I were to characterize his conversion in any other terms. In the last analysis the question of whether or not a further explanation is required is simply a matter of whether the description includes reference to a claim that can be shown to be false on independent grounds.[12]

I should be quick to point out, of course, that Proudfoot would most likely accept everything that I have said and that much of this picture is simply the result of my attempt to make more explicit points raised by Proudfoot himself throughout his book. There is no reason to deny that a subject's description of an action or experience often requires further elucidation and that this sometimes calls for what Proudfoot terms explanation. According to the picture presented above, for instance, explanations of practices, beliefs, and experiences are perfectly legitimate and are authorized on an ad hoc basis except in those cases, for example, when we have good reason to suspect that the description or attribution includes a claim that is false. For instance, there would be no prima facie reason to question the person who claims to be tormented by a headache whereas further explanation is obviously required if the description of the headache makes reference to demons in the brain. In this kind of case an explanation is clearly justified, not by virtue of a distinction between two kinds of reduction, but simply on the merits of the specific case in question.

Once again, if Proudfoot invokes the distinction between descriptive and explanatory reduction simply as a way of granting the possibility of cases such as these, there is no reason to deny the insight it affords. However, it is one thing to claim that explanations are sometimes required to make sense out of a problematic case and quite another to assume, as Proudfoot often does, that descriptions of religious experiences always entail claims that are false, namely, claims about supernatural entities, and that *for this reason* a further social scientific explanation of such experience will always be required.

The point I would like to emphasize, however, is that *there is no reason to suspect that everyone will require a further explanation of religious experience.* If, for example, I am a theist, I would have no prima facie reason to suspect that the reports of conversion experiences stand in need of any further explanation. This is because such experiences do not present the theist with the kind of puzzle or riddle that is the occasion for additional elucidation. In order to highlight this point, we might want to appeal to the work of Ludwig Wittgenstein who makes a similar observation concerning the notion of doubt in his book *On Certainty.* According to Wittgenstein, the skeptic who doubts everything cannot make this epistemological obsession intelligible for the simple reason that radical doubt would throw into question the very context that makes doubt reasonable. In other words, doubts, like beliefs, must be justified. In a similar way, one might suggest that the need for an explanation of human beliefs, practices, and experiences requires "justification" in some sense and can only be made intelligible within a certain context.

This is particularly important in the case of Proudfoot's analysis since the need for a social scientific explanation can only arise to the extent that certain kinds of commitments and priorities frame a person's particular agenda. Unfortunately, Proudfoot's discussion obscures the fact that the need to look for explanations is relative to the context in question, as I argued above, and sometimes creates the false impression that there is a *general* presumption in favor of explanatory reduction. This, however, is simply not the case. On the contrary, the demand for explanation arises only for those who have certain kinds of theoretical commitments and priorities that lead them to suspect that there is something in the agent's description of his or her experience that they cannot accept. So there can never be a *general* presumption in favor of explanatory reduction as a policy for the simple reason that such explanations are motivated by commitments and priorities not everyone might share.

Explanation then is a perfectly legitimate enterprise and requires no philosophical defense. As Wittgenstein reminds us, the activity of giving and demanding explanations is a basic activity or language game which, like other activities such as issuing commands, counting, and praying, does not require any philosophical justification. This does not mean, of course, that we do not have criteria for assessing the validity of specific explanations or for determining whether or not an explanation is required in a particular case. The point, rather, is that these matters can only be addressed by looking at the specific features of the case in question, which will include reference to the commitments and concerns that inform our investigation.

D. *Reduction and the Ethics of Belief*

Perhaps the best way to articulate the differences between thinkers such as Phillips and Winch, on the one hand, and Proudfoot on the other, is to suggest that, in the end, their conflicting views of religion are motivated by the differing commitments, priorities, and concerns that inform their respective projects. This, of course, might sound like a platitude, but it is, I think, an important platitude that can help us understand why the arguments of those who disagree about religion are often intractable. On the one hand, Phillips and Winch express a valid concern when they ask whether certain explanatory strategies can sometimes blind us to the importance of religion in human life. In this regard it is perhaps important to remind ourselves that neither Phillips nor Winch deny that understanding religion requires the ability to draw comparisons between religion and other dimensions of human life. That is, this activity of drawing analogies is an essential part of any attempt to understand religion. What both deny is simply that the best analogy is the analogy between religion and science. Instead, they focus on the way religious beliefs and practices illuminate and lend significance to perennial and enigmatic dimensions of human life such as birth, sex, and death, what Winch calls "limit notions."[13] The hope is that attention to these aspects of human life will open new possibilities for our understanding of religion.

As already mentioned, both Phillips and Winch appeal to the work of Wittgenstein to defend their views concerning religion, a fact that should come as no surprise given Wittgenstein's sympathetic views concerning such issues. Unfortunately, however, both thinkers invite criticism when they appropriate Wittgenstein's writings on religion in such a way as to create the impression that his objections to reduction are motivated by worries about rationality. This is particularly disappointing since their more insightful criticisms of reduction are based on wider considerations and reflect a tacit awareness that Wittgenstein's fundamental objections to reductionism are *ethical* ones, in the broad sense of the term.

In his "Remarks on Frazer's *The Golden Bough,*" for instance, Wittgenstein complains that Frazer's analysis of myth and ritual fails to do justice to the depth and importance of religion in human life. Although he sometimes seems to suggest that his criticism of Frazer is based simply on a fear that reduction distorts the data, a closer reading of the text reveals that his concerns are more substantive. Rather, the general worry that motivates his observations is his suspicion that a "scientific" approach to religion tends to erode our religious sensibilities and that it therefore undermines what Wittgenstein considers to be an essential dimension of human life. So although Wittgenstein himself often confesses throughout his writings that he finds it difficult to believe the specific claims of any particular religion, he suspects that our lives become spiritually and morally impoverished without some appreciation and respect for religious beliefs and practices. In short, since such beliefs and practices reflect something important about what it means to be a human being, it is morally objectionable to assume, as Frazer sometimes does, that it would be desirable to disabuse ourselves of our religious feelings and sentiments.

The problem with Frazer's approach, suggests Wittgenstein, is his tacit assumption, shared by many of his Victorian contemporaries, that religious beliefs are either false or mere prejudices to be overcome by the proper scientific training. The question Wittgenstein asks, however, is whether what appears to be an enthusiasm for scientific progress is merely an expression of the spiritlessness of the age. As Wittgenstein himself suggests in a rather Kierkegaardian remark: "What a narrow spiritual life on Frazer's part! As a result: how impossible it was for him to conceive a life different from that of the England of his time!"[14] Admittedly, it is hard to ignore the *ad hominum* nature of this observation, but neither can we deny that it expresses an important insight about the relationship between a person's spiritual character and his or her capacity to appreciate beliefs and practices he or she may not share. It is, moreover, such a connection that leads Wittgenstein to suspect that our ability to understand religion is not so much a matter of constructing a hypothesis to explain the belief or practice as it is a matter of cultivating an ability to see how such beliefs and practices might be connected with our lives.

When, for example, Wittgenstein speaks of the Beltane Fire Festival, he insists that an *explanation* cannot possibly help us understand why such rituals impress us as "deep and sinister business."[15] Unfortunately, however, it is just this kind of mistaken assumption that leads some to suggest that our feelings and responses to such practices are simply a function of our beliefs concerning their origins. Wittgenstein wonders, however, whether this assumption makes any sense or whether it just compounds the confusion. Is it always the case, for example, that our responses to such activities depend simply on whether we believe that a certain explanation of their origins is true or false? Wittgenstein himself denies that this could possibly be the case for the simple reason that our impressions of the ritual need not change, even though we were to discover that the explanation is false. As Wittgenstein suggests: "Compared with the impression which the description makes on us, the explanation is too uncertain."[16] In other words, even though we are aware that particular explanations can be revised in light of new evidence, we sense that our impressions of the ritual go deeper and are not open to revision in the same way. But if an explanation cannot account for the depth of our impression, then, suggests Wittgenstein, "one part of our account would still be missing, namely, that which brings this picture into connection with our own feelings and thoughts. This part gives the account its depth."[17]

Our capacity to understand religious beliefs and rituals, therefore, is not primarily a matter of our ability to explain their origins for the simple reason that such explanations could never account for the depth of our impression and the claim such forms of life make on us. What is needed to understand religion, rather, is two things. First of all, we require the kind of practical interpretative skills and capacities that enable us to describe the practices and rituals in a meaningful way. As a way of emphasizing this point, Wittgenstein appeals to the notion of *perspicuous representation*, an idea first introduced and developed by him in his early work on logic. As Wittgenstein says: "The concept of perspicuous representation is of fundamental importance. It denotes the form of our representation, the way we see things."[18] The task then is *not* to offer an explanation, but to assemble the facts in a certain way in order to *see* what kind of pattern might emerge: "The perspicuous representation brings about the understanding which consists precisely in the fact that we 'see the connections.' Hence the importance of finding *connecting links.*"[19]

Wittgenstein, however, is quite clear that something more is needed than the kind of skill required to produce a perspicuous representation. For this reason he suggests that there is a second dimension to this process of making the connections that requires an appeal to one's experience. That is, understanding a religion is not complete until one can make the connection with one's own feelings and thoughts. Wittgenstein summarizes these concerns in the following observation:

> I want to say: The deep, the sinister, do not depend on the history of the practice having been like this, for perhaps it was not like this at all; nor on the fact that it was perhaps or probably like this, but rather on that which gives me grounds for assuming this. . . . No, the deep and the sinister do not become apparent merely by our coming to know the history of the external action, rather it is *we* who ascribe them from an experience of our own.[20]

At first glance, of course, it might be tempting to interpret a remark such as this as an appeal to some kind of inner intuition, such as we find in the early work of Friedrich Schleiermacher or in the writings of Rudolf Otto, both of whom seem to base their views of religion on a kind of naive romantic epistemology.[21] The problem with this view, however, is that it runs contrary to the entire spirit of Wittgenstein's later philosophy of mind where we find his well-known and sustained polemic against any such appeal to the idea of "inner intuitions." For this reason, it might be more helpful to interpret this passage as a reminder that a person's understanding of religion presupposes that he or she has already undergone the appropriate spiritual training and formation. In more Wittgensteinian terms, understanding religion presupposes an ability to make the appropriate connections with one's own experience and a person becomes able to make the relevant connections to the extent that one has some familiarity with this particular form of life. In the end then there is no reason to suspect that Wittgenstein's appeal to experience as a necessary condition for understanding religion trades on the kind of naive and unacceptable appeals to intuition we find in some writers such as Schleiermacher and Otto.

At this point I would like to suggest that Wittgenstein's objections to Frazer stem from his suspicion that his kind of approach would be inimical to the type of formation necessary to understand how religion can be "deep and sinister business." Beginning with the assumption that religious life is based on ignorance and superstition, Frazer appeals to scientific approaches with the hope that they will undermine our capacity to make the relevant "existential" connections. But unless we can make the relevant "existential" connections, we will not have the ability to understand an essential dimension of our heritage as human beings. And if there is any doubt that Wittgenstein believes that religion is an essential part of our natural history, we should remind ourselves that he himself admits as much when he says there might be some truth to the view that we are "religious animals": "One could almost say that man is a ceremonial animal. That is, no doubt, partly wrong and partly nonsensical, but there is also something right about it. . . ."[22]

No doubt, Wittgenstein comes very close to making the controversial suggestion that our species might be characterized as *homo religiosus*, a claim advanced by historian of religions Mircea Eliade throughout his writings. Wittgenstein's caveat, however, should lead us to suspect that he wishes to be much more circumspect in his claim. In particular, Wittgenstein would want to eschew the mistake of those who assume that any reference to *homo religiosus* also legitimates, in some strange way, talk about supernatural entities or worse yet, something about the essence of human beings. In this sense, Wittgenstein never strays from the path of his own austere and uncompromising agnosticism. By the same token, however, Wittgenstein does seem to think that our capacity to experience religious emotions and feelings is not simply something determined by our particular culture. He is, of course, well aware that the particular beliefs and experiences of any group of people will be shaped according to their shared practices and language. But this does not rule out the stronger claim, implicit in Wittgenstein's remarks on Frazer, that the capacity to share in such a form of life presupposes primitive responses such as awe, love, and fear and thus reflects what it means to be human.[23]

In this respect, a remark made by Wittgenstein in his *Philosophical Investigations* can serve as a commentary on his claim that religious practices and beliefs reveal something important about the kind of creatures we are: "What we are supplying are really remarks on the natural history of human beings; we are not contributing curiosities, however, but observations which no one has doubted, but which have escaped remark only because they are always before our eyes."[24] Like certain primitive responses such as benevolence, which writers such as David Hume rightly assume to be the basis for any language of morals,[25] Wittgenstein would insist that religion is not simply a linguistic artifact, as many so-called Wittgensteinians would have us assume. It is rather a shared form of life that is essential to our understanding of ourselves as human beings. For this reason, a failure to understand ourselves as religious creatures is a sign that we have become impoverished as human beings. As such, this kind of failure is not an epistemic but an *ethical* one.

E. Concluding Remarks

In the end the differences between these two positions concerning reduction reflect contrasting but valid insights concerning the conditions for the possibility of understanding religion, to use a Kantian turn of phrase. Proudfoot's account can prove as an essential reminder that in some contexts explanations of religion might be perfectly justified, even though it is a mistake, I think, to suppose that we defend explanatory reductionism as a *general* strategy to be employed by *everyone* in their attempts to understand religion. As I have already suggested, an approach such as Proudfoot's is especially helpful when one's prior commitments and concerns make it impossible to accept the truth of religious claims. In fact, in cases such as these, an appeal to explanation might be the only way to make sense of experiences that would otherwise remain unintelligible.

Phillips and Winch, however, would want to warn us that there is a price to be paid by following Proudfoot's approach. The need to render our lives intelligible is inexorable and explanation is simply the expression of this natural drive to understand. The risk, however, is that the desire to make the experiences of others intelligible to us by appealing only to categories familiar to us could blind us to other possibilities for understanding human life. As Winch himself suggests: "Seriously to study another way of life is necessarily to seek to extend our own."[26] In fact, there might even be times when such study might lead us to abandon what we once considered to be our most cherished beliefs and to appropriate radically new categories for understanding ourselves and the world. Only in this way can we allow for the possibility that the Azande witch doctor might abandon his traditional beliefs and acquire a modern skeptical attitude about magic. Nor should we forget the case of the anthropologist who abandons the secular world of academia to become a Buddhist monk.[27] Traditionally, Christians have explored the dynamics of this kind of change under the rubric of conversion. The lesson is clear: we must make sure that our philosophical and theoretical commitments allow for such possibilities.

One of my major concerns throughout this book has been to do justice to both viewpoints explored in this chapter and to suggest that the ethics of belief is primarily a matter of our ability and willingness to balance trust and confidence in our basic concerns and commitments with a willingness to entertain new ideas that might call our previous way of looking at the world into question. This is not to deny, of course, that there are limits that constrain our ability to achieve and maintain this kind of balance. There are, of course, moral limitations as well as limits of a more practical kind. Without some degree of confidence that our way of looking at the world is relatively stable and secure, our lives would be meaningless. But it is precisely this practical confidence in our way of looking at the world that secures the intellectual courage necessary to explore strange and alien ways of life.

Notes

1. *The Complete Poems of Emily Dickinson*, ed. Thomas H. Johnson (Boston: Little Brown and Company, 1960), no. 165.

2. Perhaps his most important contribution to the debate is the essay "On the Very Idea of a Conceptual Scheme," *Inquiries into Truth and Interpretation* (Oxford: Clarendon Press, 1984), pp. 183–98.

3. D. Z. Phillips, *Religion without Explanation* (Oxford: Basil Blackwell, 1976).

4. Ibid., p. 7.

5. Ibid., p. 30.

6. Ibid., p. 62.

7. Peter Winch, *The Idea of a Social Science* (London: Routledge and Kegan Paul, 1958).

8. Peter Winch, "Understanding a Primitive Society," in *Ethics and Action* (London: Routledge and Kegan Paul, 1972), p. 12. This essay has also appeared in many anthologies, most notably *Rationality*, ed. Bryan R. Wilson (Oxford: Basil Blackwell, 1970), pp. 78–111.

9. See, for example, Alasdair MacIntyre, "The Idea of a Social Science," in *Rationality*, pp. 112–30, as well as his "Is Understanding Religion Compatible with Believing?" in the same volume, pp. 62–77.

10. Perhaps one of the more unfortunate aspects of the relativism debate is the tendency of many talented philosophers to spend an inordinate amount of time and energy rehearsing over and over again Davidson's insightful criticism. Although few people still worry about the problem of the "translatability of natural languages," some still suspect that this dead horse is not quite dead enough. For the latest contribution to the sempiternal crusade against relativism see Jeffrey Stout's *Ethics After Babel*.

11. Wayne Proudfoot, *Religious Experience* (Berkeley: University of California Press, 1985).

12. Similar worries concerning explanation and religious experience are voiced by Gary Gutting in his *Religious Belief and Religious Skepticism* (Notre Dame: University of Notre Dame Press, 1982), esp. pp. 158–77.

13. See, for example, Winch's enlightening discussion of these issues in "Understanding a Primitive Society," pp. 43ff.

14. Ludwig Wittgenstein, "Remarks on Frazer's *The Golden Bough*," in *Wittgenstein: Sources and Perspectives*, ed. C. G. Luckhardt (Sussex: The Harvester Press, 1979), p. 65.

15. Ibid., p. 77.

16. Ibid., p. 63.

17. Ibid., p. 74.

18. Ibid., p. 69.

19. Ibid.

20. Ibid., p. 77.

21. Criticisms of "romantic religion," understood in this classic sense, underlie the current trend in the study of religion to adopt a more

linguistic approach to these issues. An excellent example of this kind of proposal is Proudfoot's book, which can be read as a sustained critique of appeals to romantic epistemology in the study of religion. Among theologians such as Karl Barth, criticisms of romantic epistemology have traditionally been motivated as prolegomena to a more general critique of theological liberalism. The latest example of this kind of proposal that makes explicit reference to the work of Wittgenstein is George Lindbeck, The *Nature of Doctrine: Religion and Theology in a Postliberal Age* (Philadelphia: The Westminster Press, 1984), esp. pp. 30–45.

22. Wittgenstein, "Remarks on Frazer's *The Golden Bough*," p. 67.

23. My reading of Wittgenstein on these points has been shaped by Rodger Beehler's *Moral Life* (Totowa: Rowman and Littlefield, 1978). Beehler's Humean insight involves the claim that moral language would have no place in human life if we did not demonstrate those primitive responses, such as caring, which are part of our natural history. Beehler's appropriation of Wittgenstein serves as an important corrective to the "language fetishism" that sometimes characterizes Wittgenstein scholarship. Another thinker who has insightfully appropriated Wittgenstein in her discussion of David Hume is Annette Baier, *Postures of the Mind: Essays on Mind and Morals* (Minneapolis: University of Minnesota Press, 1985).

24. Ludwig Wittgenstein, *Philosophical Investigations*, trans. G. E. M. Anscombe (New York: Macmillan Company, 1958), sec. 415.

25. David Hume, *An Inquiry Concerning the Principles of Morals* (Indianapolis: Hackett Publishing, 1983), pp. 16–20.

26. Winch, "Understanding a Primitive Society," p. 33.

27. I have been reminded of the validity of such concerns in numerous conversations with Kevin Trainor.

8

Between Objectivity and Subjectivity: The Life of Irony

If the fundamental question of morality is "How should I live?" then the basic question of the ethics of belief concerns analogous questions; namely, "How should I think?" and "What should I believe?" As we have seen, many thinkers from John Locke to Anthony Flew have expressed a particular interest in how a person should govern his or her religious beliefs and have proposed certain rules and principles to regulate these epistemic activities. Locke, for example, troubled by the religious enthusiasts of his time, begins with the claim that a people are entitled to hold their beliefs only if they can be justified by an appeal to neutral epistemic criteria. Locke himself, of course, was a theist and not surprisingly expresses confidence that theism and Christianity are defensible. It was not long though before other thinkers, from Enlightenment figures such as David Hume to Victorian critics of religion such as W. K. Clifford and Leslie Stephen, among others, turned these assumptions against the theists in order to undermine their religious claims. By the middle of the nineteenth century, critiques of religion became even more polemical as the great critics of religion such as Karl Marx, Sigmund Freud, Arthur Schopenhauer, and Friedrich Nietzsche, to name the more well-known ones, took the offensive and sharpened their attacks against Christianity. The story is, of course, a commonplace and has undoubtedly become part of our cultural legacy.

The question, however, is whether the assumptions underlying the traditional picture of the ethics of belief can be defended and whether believers have any other options. As we have seen, thinkers such as Samuel Coleridge and John Henry Newman, troubled by the implications of Lockean empiricism, offer convincing arguments in favor of what Michael Polanyi calls "personal knowledge." Convinced that there are no good reasons why personal considerations of piety should not inform

our reflections concerning Christian epistemology, Coleridge and Newman assume that the reasons a person actually offers in defense of his or
her religious convictions are "theory-laden," and will therefore most
likely involve appeals to religious considerations such as feelings of guilt
or sin-consciousness, and a desire for salvation. Both argue, quite rightly
in my view, that it is a mistake to expect that people should defend their
beliefs by an appeal to neutral epistemic considerations, especially
when the "real" reasons that ground a person's religious beliefs are religious ones.

The problem with this approach to the ethics of belief, however, is
that it does not address how an individual's concerns about guilt or sin
might be motivated. After all, as both Coleridge and Newman admit, not
everyone will be led to construe and assess their lives in these terms. Such
worries, as we have seen, lead certain thinkers such as Søren Kierkegaard
and Ludwig Wittgenstein to suggest that it is not enough to ask whether
a person's religious beliefs are justified in some minimal sense. On the
contrary, one must first explore the ways such beliefs can be viewed as interpretations about the meaning of life. To say, for example, that some
people assess the shape of their lives with reference to concepts such as
sin, justification, and sanctification is to say, with Wittgenstein, that
they have different pictures that enable them to see their lives as meaningful wholes. Socialized into different communities with differing
stories about the place and significance of human life in the cosmos,
human beings appeal to a wide range of rituals and symbols to answer
the ultimate questions about the meaning of it all—the meaning of
birth, love, suffering, and death.

We have seen, however, that if religious beliefs are best viewed as interpretations about the meaning of life, then there is no good reason to
expect people will reach agreement about these differing solutions to the
dilemma of existence. As I suggested in my brief discussion of David
Wiggins, since religious beliefs involve judgments about the meaning of
life, they are cognitively underdetermined, which is another way of saying that they fall short of plain truth. Some, such as Konstanin Levin in
Tolstoy's *Anna Karenina*, will answer the riddle in theistic terms. Others,
such as Ingmar Bergman's character Tomas Erikson, will sometimes discover that they can no longer make sense of their lives in religious terms,
even though they might try to evade this realization by appealing to subtle strategies of self-deception. Because such beliefs are cognitively underdetermined and interact in complex and subtle ways with a person's
desires, intentions, and emotions, they are particularly vulnerable. In
the end, there is no way to predict or specify in advance the many ways
they can be put at risk.

Unfortunately, many philosophers of religion tend to ignore this feature of religious belief and therefore fail to acknowledge the fragility of faith. As we have seen, this tendency can be found in the work of reformed epistemologists such as Alvin Plantinga who, in his Free Will Defense, fails to account for the way a person's responses to the problem of evil implicate their characters in an important way. Characters such as Ivan Karamazov should serve as important reminders that the assessment of a person's beliefs about these ultimate issues must take the broader picture into account. The fact that both theists and atheists often devise elaborate strategies that blind them to alternative ways of viewing the problem of evil should lead us to consider seriously what Simone Weil has said about the issue. For this reason, I have argued that a renewed appreciation of the virtue of attention can help remedy the vice of blindness that afflicts theists and atheists alike.

Not surprisingly, such concerns are not limited to the philosophy of religion; all students of religion must confront similiar worries about the scope and limits of critical self-reflection and the challenges posed by the problem of reductionism. Once again, we have seen that in a context such as this, the task is to balance the commitments and theoretical priorities that one brings to the study of religion with a degree of critical flexibility. In the debate between antireductionists such as D. Z. Phillips and reductionists such as Wayne Proudfoot, the argument generally revolves around concerns about rationality and relativism. As I have tried to show, however, Wittgenstein's critique of Frazer provides us with a different picture which sees reductionism as an ethical concern. For if, as Wittgenstein suggests, religion forms an essential part of our natural history as human beings, we should be wary of reductionistic strategies for "understanding" religion to the extent that they erode and undermine our respect for the place of religion in our form of life.

What then does this mean with respect to the ethics of belief? I hope that it has become clear throughout this discussion that rules and principles are of little use when we ask the question "How shall I think?" or "What shall I believe?" In the end, the lesson is that it is a mistake to treat the ethics of belief primarily as an epistemological concern. Because questions about the point and significance of a person's or community's religious beliefs are tied to the attempt to find meaning in life, it might be best to say that even the distinction between the question "What should I believe?" and "How should I live?" might lead us astray. If the ethics of belief is basically a practical question about what a person values and cares about, we should not be surprised to learn that there is no algorithm to help us sort out these concerns. In short, the stance people take with respect to their religious beliefs cannot be assessed independently of those basic values and commitments that enable them to make sense of their lives as a meaningful whole.

At first glance it might seem that the picture I have proposed is a concession to irrationality and intellectual chaos. For if one's epistemic standards cannot be articulated independently of one's practical interests and wider concerns about the meaning of life, there no longer appear to be any "objective" criteria whereby a person can govern or assess one's basic commitments. There is, I confess, some truth to this objection, but on closer examination the worries turn out to be quite innocuous, if only because they turn on a misunderstanding about terms such as "subjectivity" and "objectivity."

Unfortunately, it is very common to appeal to terms such as "subjectivity" and "objectivity" in the course of discussion or debate even though we often have no clear idea of what these terms mean. Undoubtedly, they seem to fulfill a basic polemical purpose and for this reason we rarely take the time to examine what we mean when we say, for instance, that an argument is not sound because the facts on which it is based are merely "subjective." The motivation underlying such objections is the assumption that if someone's facts are merely "subjective" then there is no reason to take that position seriously. Not surprisingly, we tend to hurl such epithets at our opponents only when we sense that we have reached an impass and that our disagreement seems intractable. In one sense, I think that this is a perfectly natural response to the frustration we feel from time to time when our conversation partners do not seem to see the point of our position. Perhaps it might be helpful though to explore the roots of this frustration in more detail to see whether we can gain some insight into the elusive terms "subjectivity" and "objectivity."

Perhaps the first thing to note about these terms is that we often but quite mistakenly use them to assess "facts." As Max Deutscher has recently pointed out, however, this common tendency is based on a confusion.[1] To say, for example, that a fact is "objective" might give the impression that it is more acceptable or reliable than its weaker rival, the mere "subjective" fact. A closer look though, says Deutscher, will show that the qualification "objective" or "subjective" does not add anything to our understanding of the fact of the matter. Very simply, a fact is a fact is a fact. To say that a fact is objective may produce the illusion that we have said something more—that perhaps our claim is more in accord with the way things are. In the end this rhetorical strategy is a chimera that only reinforces the tacit dogmatism of those who appeal to the "objectivity" of their "facts" in order to protect them from objections.

But if "objectivity" and "subjectivity" are not criteria for the assessment of facts, what purchase do they have in the economy of debate and discussion? Deutscher argues at length that the best way to understand these two elusive terms is to view them as ways of appraising a person's *style* of thinking. According to Deutscher, who never himself uses the phrase "ethics of belief," the terms "objectivity" and "subjectivity" are basically criteria for assessing a person's intellectual character. This claim, developed at length in Deutscher's interesting and important book, *Subjecting and Objecting,* is especially relevant to the question of whether there is anything we can say about the stance a person takes with respect to his or her religious beliefs.

According to Deutscher, much of the debate that has motivated discussion about "subjectivity" and "objectivity" is based on certain myths and fantasies that underlie our quest for knowledge. Perhaps the most misguided view, says Deutscher, is the claim that "subjectivity" and "objectivity" are shorthand for two mutually exclusive ways of viewing the world. On the one hand, we have the skeptic who insists that everyone is bound and limited by one's own subjective perspective. When such people are confronted by views and beliefs they might not share, the tendency is to protect their convictions from any challenge with the flat-footed defense that "everything is subjective." On the other hand, there are those who place a premium on objectivity and therefore are suspicious whenever they sense that others are defending their views by an appeal to "subjective" considerations. For the advocate of this kind of radical objectivism, any concession to mere subjective considerations is bound to be seen as a symptom of woolly-headed complacency, or worse, downright irrationality.

Deutscher himself is suspicious of the way this debate has been formulated and argues at length that even though it appears that we have two mutually opposing views, this impression is based on a false dilemma. Although a short synopsis cannot possibly do justice to Deutscher's lively and convincing discussion of this question, it is clear that he wants to split the difference between these two positions and to suggest instead that "subjecting" and "objecting" are two interdependent processes that describe the various ways we come to terms with the world. He suggests that it is a mistake to think that we can escape from our particular commitments, concerns, priorities, and interests. We must avoid the tempting but confused claim that the only knowledge worth having is a knowledge that is nobody's in particular—that perhaps we can step out of our skins and view the world from the standpoint of absolute objectivity. As Deutscher remarks at one point, we might characterize "suicide as perfect objectivity."[2]

Clearly then any knowledge worth having is knowledge that will be motivated by our involvements. But does this mean that we are doomed to a blind subjectivism from which we cannot escape? By no means. For the most part, Deutscher's intriguing essay is a defense of objectivity and for this reason he wants to maintain that we can acknowledge the fact that our knowledge is perspectival without succumbing to the despair of epistemological solipsism. The key, says Deutscher, is not to renounce our subjectivity, but to cultivate a style of thinking that allows for the kind of flexibility required for "objecting." As Deutscher himself suggests:

> To dismiss all objectivity because of our inevitable subjective involvement is like declaring null and void the culinary arts, the sharing of food around a table, and the use of bowls, chopsticks, knives and forks because without hunger and the need for food there would be no sense in any cultivated practices of preparing, sharing and eating food. Objectivity is an intelligent learned use of our subjectivity, not an escape from it.[3]

Of particular importance is Deutscher's Wittgensteinian suggestion that objectivity is not to be construed as a flight from finitude. In fact, what makes human knowledge possible is the fact that the possibilities for human understanding are circumscribed by our human, all too human, point of view. What is needed, as Deutscher says, is not an escape from subjectivity, but rather what he calls an "intelligent learned use of our subjectivity." Ironically, both the radical subjectivist and the dogmatic objectivist fail to realize the possibility that human knowing demands a capacity to appreciate and appropriate "subjecting" and "objecting" as interrelated ways of coming to terms with reality.

At first glance, it might appear as if Deutscher's proposal, though suggestive, offers us precious little with respect to concrete guidelines that might enable us to cultivate and maintain this difficult balance. Indeed, the person who is looking for solid principles or some decision procedure that might ensure this delicate balance is likely to be disappointed with his recommendations. This worry, however, should not bother us for the simple reason that a person's ability to negotiate the balance between subjectivity and objectivity does not depend on the application of rules or principles. As Deutscher rightly suggests, the ethics of belief is primarily a matter of a person's intellectual character.

Not surprisingly then, Deutscher articulates his understanding of what I call the ethics of belief in terms of those virtues and vices that enable one to maintain a mean between the vices of blind dogmatism and rootless skepticism. Of particular interest is Deutscher's claim that the cultivation of intelligent objectivity requires a self-critical awareness of the many ways our particular thoughts, interests, and emotions color the way we view the world. This does not mean, of course, that we should strive to become detached and emotionless. Nor does it mean that subjectivity is a necessary evil. Such a misguided view of objectivity is based on the fallacious and hyperrationalistic assumption that our interests and emotions necessarily lead to a distorted view of reality. On the contrary, it is probably closer to the truth to say that emotions play an essential role in our attempts to acquire knowledge about the world.[4] Our emotions pose no threat to objectivity for the simple reason that they constitute a person's particular perspective that defines what things are worthy of his or her attention. The task then is not to repress or eliminate our emotions, for without emotions objectivity would be impossible. The point instead is that objectivity demands the intelligent and skillful appropriation of these emotions. As Deutscher himself maintains: "The getting of objectivity and the holding on to it require emotions of curiosity, love, hate, desire and fear, as much as they require the moments of crucial control and restraint in the expression and harnessed use of these emotions."[5]

The greatest threat to objectivity, suggests Deutscher, is not our emotions, but rather the vices of a self-absorbed outlook that prevent us from coming to terms with reality. Although we tend to think of "vices" primarily as ways of characterizing a person's moral life, it is clear that these moral shortcomings are also responsible for many of our intellectual failings. A good example that Deutscher explores in some detail is the vice of vanity, which we tend to view simply as a flaw in one's social or moral character. What we often overlook, however, is the extent to which vanity undermines our capacity to assess critically our own views and beliefs. Unlike the autonomous person, whose practical self-confidence is balanced by an interest in critical self-appraisal, the vain person refuses to consider other points of view. What makes vanity particularly perverse is that people who are vain are motivated to maintain their beliefs for the simple reason that they are *their* beliefs. The intellectual life corrupted by vanity is guided by a peculiar maxim that privileges one's point of view simply because it is one's own: "Of course this view is correct—it is, after all, *my* belief, isn't it?"

Vanity is just one of the many vices that undermine our ability to cultivate the intelligent appropriation of subjectivity and objectivity. The picture becomes even more complicated when we consider the various other vices that prevent us from acquiring a confident but flexible intellectual character. In addition to self-deception and reductionism, both of which we have already explored in some detail, there is the kind of intellectual blindness that accompanies other vices such as arrogance, envy, and jealousy, all of which Deutscher examines throughout his book. Without exploring these vices in more detail, it is fair to say that they are detrimental to the life of intellectual virtue to the extent they are symptomatic of the kind of self-absorbed outlook that characterizes the person preoccupied with preserving, at all costs, his or her beliefs and convictions. What is needed, however, is not a contempt for one's subjectivity. As already mentioned, one's interests, concerns, and emotions define in an important way each person's unique contribution to debate and discussion. The key, rather, is the virtue of self-confidence that welcomes new possibilities for understanding our lives.

The value of an analysis such as Deutscher's then lies in the guiding intuition that the question "What or how should I believe?" cannot be answered without reference to the more general question, "How should I live?" The problem with most traditional approaches to the ethics of belief is that they tend to overlook the extent to which our epistemic failures arise from failures of character. Even when thinkers openly acknowledge their suspicion that the ethics of belief is primarily an ethical concern, they often proceed as if the problem can be solved by an appeal to some method or decision procedure for ensuring our knowledge. We have seen, for example, that even though Locke realizes that our intellectual failings are often the result of wishful thinking, a desire to believe what we want to believe, and misguided enthusiasm, he still hopes that a theory of knowledge might solve the problem. Clearly, there are times when our epistemic failures are due to mistakes and conceptual confusions. It would be a mistake to deny that in such cases the reasoned arguments of the philosophers might help us find our way through dark and rugged terrain. We must not forget, however, that in those cases in which our epistemic failures are tied to general flaws in our character, we might require a quite different cure.

How then are we to avoid those vices that compromise our intellectual character and undermine our ability to balance our subjective perspective with the claims of objectivity? In order to answer this question, I would like to conclude by turning once again to the work of Ralph Waldo Emerson whose enigmatic remarks concerning his own spiritual journey suggest that the ethics of belief is primarily a matter of one's *style* of thinking. Like his contemporaries Søren Kierkegaard and Friedrich Nietzsche, Emerson wishes to call our attention to a more holistic way of understanding our intellectual lives. Wary of the philosophical prejudice that identifies serious thinking with *justification*, Emerson manages to avoid this kind of reductionism by insisting that existential concerns, such as finding meaning in one's life, must be explored in a more pragmatic fashion. The result of his own reflections, what I like to term Emersonian pragmatism, is a picture of the intellectual life that promotes self-trust without compromising the creative flexibility of a healthy skepticism. In short, this pragmatism reflects a style of thinking about our lives that attempts to strike the difficult balance between "subjectivity" and "objectivity."

In his well-known essay "Circles," Emerson characterizes this type of existential pragmatism in general terms when he suggests that "our life is an apprenticeship to the truth, that around every circle another can be drawn. . . ."[6] As he develops this theme throughout the essay, it becomes quite clear that he wishes to promote the idea that a person's life is a never-ending journey of discovery and invention. In this respect, the metaphor of the circle, to which he appeals throughout the essay, is quite appropriate. First of all, inquiry, like the circumference of a circle, has neither a beginning nor an end. More importantly, however, is Emerson's allusion to conversation as a game of circles,[7] which suggests that there is, in principle, no limit to a person's ongoing quest for self-understanding: "The life of man is a self-evolving circle, which, from a ring imperceptibly small, rushes on all sides outwards to new and larger circles, and that without end."[8] To speak of life as an apprenticeship to the truth then is to endorse the Emersonian hope that conversation will always provide new opportunities for reinterpreting our lives.

There is, however, no venture without risk. Emerson is well aware that the type of existential pragmatism he celebrates throughout his writings can sometimes lead to the erosion of one's basic commitments and concerns. In particular, if one regards oneself as an apprentice to the truth, one must be prepared to discover new and unexpected paradigms for self-interpretation, even when they challenge one's fundamental beliefs. This is not to say, of course, that the apprentice to truth should have no confidence in his or her particular way of viewing the world. What it does mean, however, is that there are no arguments or justifications that can *secure* one's faith in one's basic commitments. But if this is the case, it is always possible that the Emersonian thinker will find it necessary to abandon old ways of construing his or her basic concerns in favor of new and more illuminating self-interpretations: "In the thought of to-morrow there is a power to upheave all thy creed, all the creeds, all the literatures of the nations, and marshal thee to a heaven which no epic dream has yet depicted." [9]

Like his contemporary Søren Kierkegaard, who insists that a person's freedom to constitute himself is always the occasion of *angest* or dread, Emerson acknowledges that the task of becoming a self is a precarious enterprise. For although the endless play of possible self-interpretations can be quite liberating, the lack of closure can also be terrifying. Unlike Kierkegaard, however, whose pseudonyms appeal to nuanced psychological analyses to explain the possibility of this dread, Emerson paints a stark picture of the self seeking to find some basis for confidence in face of the unknown. Consider the haunting passage at the beginning of his essay "Experience":

> Where do we find ourselves? In a series, of which we do not
> know the extremes, and believe that it has none. We wake and

find ourselves on a stair: there are stairs below us, which we
seem to have ascended, there are stairs above us, many a one,
which go upward and out of sight . . .[10]

The vertigo that we experience when we realize that there are no foundations to ensure the stability of the self contributes to our sense of uncertainty. The task, however, is to realize that this sense of perplexity is
an unavoidable part of what it means to be an apprentice to the truth.
Not surprisingly then Emerson insists that people cannot explore new
possibilities for self-understanding unless they are willing to forgo the
security of their own parochial point of view. For there is, he says, "No
truth so sublime but it may be trivial tomorrow in the light of new
thoughts. People wish to be settled: only as far as they are unsettled, is
there any hope for them."[11]

At this point it should be clear that the open-ended free play of Emersonian pragmatism calls into question many of the basic assumptions
that underlie the theist's approach to the ethics of belief. Unlike Kierkegaard, for example, who insists that the only remedy for a person's
existential vertigo is an unconditional and unchanging commitment to
the Eternal, the Emersonian pragmatist is willing to put one's religious
convictions at risk. This is not to say, however, that Emerson would endorse the radical views of his admirer Friedrich Nietzsche, who invites
Christians to live without their beliefs in order to put their faith to the
test. Emerson's "experimentalism," developed in essays such as "Circles," is much more modest. The apprentice to the truth, according to
Emerson, is not required to repudiate his or her religious convictions in
an arbitrary fashion. Such a project is self-defeating to the extent that it
undermines in an unacceptable fashion a person's ability to make sense
of life. What Emerson does acknowledge, however, is that a person's religious beliefs are vulnerable and that the apprentice to truth must be
willing to forgo the dogmatism of the believer, such as Kierkegaard, who
insists that faith must be unconditional and unshakeable. Perhaps the
most troubling aspect of my Emersonian proposal is that it allows for the
possibility of finding it difficult to sustain one's faith in the face of new
self-interpretations that challenge one's religious convictions. Sometimes, of course, it will be possible to rethink one's beliefs in order to preserve one's identity as a Christian. By the same token, there is no reason
to expect that people will be able to sustain their faith in every situation.
Many times a loss of faith might be a person's only viable alternative.

Unlike the theist who insists that religious belief must always be
grounded on an unconditional commitment, the Emersonian pragmatist is willing to acknowledge the fragility of faith. Not surprisingly
then the apprentice to the truth is more likely to offer a more sympathet-

ic and nuanced account of what it means for a person to lose faith. In some cases, of course, it would be appropriate to grant the validity of what Kierkegaard says when he characterizes the loss or lack of faith as despair. We have seen, for example, that for Dostoyevski's famous character Ivan Karamazov atheism functions as an excuse to rationalize fundamental flaws in his personality. Indeed, one need not be a believer in order to see that Ivan's atheism lends itself to this kind of critique and to conclude that there is something terribly pernicious about his rejection of God.

By the same token, however, we must remember that even though a loss of faith can often be an expression of despair, Kierkegaard is simply wrong to insist that this is always the case. Unlike Kierkegaard, the Emersonian pragmatist is likely to approach this issue with more caution. In particular, rather than insisting that a person's loss of faith is always an expression of despair, the apprentice to truth is willing to grant that a loss of faith might be an occasion for the renewal of the practical confidence which Emerson calls "self-trust" or "self-reliance." Unlike theists such as Kierkegaard for whom the loss of religious faith necessarily entails a loss of one's self, Emerson allows for other possibilities grounded in the individual's power of self-recovery:

> Valor consists in the power of self-recovery, so that a man cannot have his flank turned, cannot be outgeneralled, but put him where you will, he stands. This can only be by his preferring truth to his past apprehension of truth; and his alert acceptance of it from whatever quarter; the intrepid conviction that his laws, his relations to society; his christianity, his world, may at any time be superseded and decease.[12]

Notwithstanding recent attempts to view Emerson's work as an exercise in traditional epistemology,[13] it is perhaps more plausible to interpret Emerson's work in more radical terms as a *critique* of epistemology. His awareness of the promise and the risks of conversation might even lead us to suggest that Emerson's work is a perfect example of what Richard Rorty has recently termed "edifying philosophy."[14] In fact, even though Rorty himself never mentions Emerson by name when he discusses edifying philosophers such as Søren Kierkegaard, William James, John Dewey, and Ludwig Wittgenstein, I think that his explication of hermeneutics and conversation in the concluding chapter of *Philosophy and the Mirror of Nature* as well as his remarks on the "Contingency of Selfhood" in *Contingency, Irony and Solidarity* are informed by the spirit of what I have called "Emersonian pragmatism."

Like Rorty, Emerson insists that the apprentice to truth must be an edifying philosopher, an all-purpose scholar who is not afraid to explore new ways of thinking about human life. For this reason, the apprentice to truth would share Rorty's suspicion of the professional philosopher who strives to secure our self-understanding with a theory of knowledge. Not only is such a project doomed to failure, as Rorty himself argues, it results in a kind of presumption that blinds us to other opportunities for making sense of our lives. Emerson warns against this kind of intellectual myopia when he observes: "Truth is an element of life, yet if a man fasten his attention on a single aspect of truth, and apply himself to that alone for a long time, the truth becomes distorted and not itself, but falsehood. . . ."[15] For this reason, Emerson endorses the example of the edifying philosopher such as Lessing who, if given the choice between truth and the lifelong pursuit of truth, would opt for the latter. Not surprisingly, we can discern an echo of Lessing's voice in Emerson's own choice to remain an apprentice to truth:

> God offers to every mind its choice between truth and repose. Take which you please,—you can never have both. Between these, as a pendulum, man oscillates. He in whom the love of repose predominates, will accept the first creed, the first philosophy, the first political party he meets,—most likely, his father's. He gets rest, commodity, and reputation; but he shuts the door of truth. He in whom the love of truth predominates, will keep himself aloof from all moorings and afloat. He will abstain from dogmatism, and recognize all the opposite negations between which, as walls, his being is swung. He submits to the inconvenience of suspense and imperfect opinion, but he is a candidate for truth, as the other is not, and respects the highest law of his being.[16]

What then can we finally say about the ethics of belief after epistemology? If there is an answer to this question, it will most likely be found in the edifying philosophy that Emerson calls an "apprenticeship to truth." But unlike traditional epistemology, this kind of reflection will have a hermeneutical dimension. It will involve a willingness to discover and explore new possibilities for understanding our lives. In addition, it will sometimes require a willingness to wait on beliefs and concerns we may not share. Finally and most importantly it will involve a willingness to put our own beliefs at risk. For in the end, the ethics of belief is nothing more than the ethics of conversation and conversion.

Notes

1. Max Deutscher, *Subjecting and Objecting* (London: Basil Blackwell, 1983), pp. 13–14.

2. Ibid., p. 17.

3. Ibid., p. 19.

4. See, for example, Ronald de Sousa, *The Rationality of Emotion* (Cambridge: MIT Press, 1987). Of particular interest is De Sousa's discussion of the "frame problem" and his suggestion that without emotions we would lack the kind of attention necessary for intelligent thought and behavior.

5. Deutscher, *Subjecting and Objecting*, p. 129.

6. Ralph Waldo Emerson, *The Essays of Ralph Waldo Emerson*, intro. Alfred Kazin (Cambridge: Belknap Press, 1987), p. 179.

7. Ibid., p. 184.

8. Ibid., p. 180.

9. Ibid., p. 181.

10. Ibid., p. 245.

11. Ibid., p. 189.

12. Ibid., p. 183.

13. See, for example, David Van Leer's recent study, *Emerson's Epistemology* (Cambridge: Cambridge University Press, 1987), which attempts to show that Emerson's enigmatic prose hides sustained and sophisticated discussions of various epistemological issues. Unfortunately, although Van Leer raises some important issues, his exposition tends to confuse rather than illuminate his provocative thesis.

14. See Richard Rorty, *Philosophy and the Mirror of Nature* (Princeton: Princeton University Press, 1979), esp. pp. 357ff.

15. "Intellect," in *The Essays of Ralph Waldo Emerson*, p. 200.

16. Ibid., p. 202.

—— Bibliography ——

Aristotle. *Nicomachean Ethics.* Translated by Terence Irwin. Indianapolis: Hackett Publishing, 1985.

Ayer, A. J. *Language, Truth and Logic.* New York: Dover Publications, 1952.

Baier, Annette. *Postures of the Mind: Essays on Mind and Morals.* Minneapolis: University of Minneapolis Press, 1985.

Barth, J. Robert, S.J. *Coleridge and Christian Doctrine.* Cambridge: Harvard University Press, 1969.

Beehler, Roger. *Moral Life.* Totowa: Rowman and Littlefield, 1978.

Bergman, Ingmar. "Winter Light." *Three Films by Ingmar Bergman.* Translated by Paul Britten Austin. New York: Grove Press, 1967.

Brockhaus, Richard R. *Pulling up the Ladder: The Metaphysical Roots of Wittgenstein's "Tractatus Logico-Philosophicus."* La Salle: Open Court, 1990.

Burnaby, J. *Amor Dei.* London: Hodder and Stoughton, 1938.

Cameron, J. M. "John Henry Newman and the Tractarian Movement." *Nineteenth Century Religious Thought in the West.* Vol. 2. Edited by Ninian Smart, John Clayton, Steven Katz, and Patrick Sherry. Cambridge: Cambridge University Press, 1985.

Carpenter, Frederic Ives. *Emerson Handbook.* New York: Hendricks House, Inc., 1953.

———. "William James and Emerson." In *On Emerson.* Edited by Edwin Cady and Louis Budd. Durham: Duke University Press, 1988.

Cavell, Stanley. *The Claim of Reason: Wittgenstein, Skepticism, Morality and Tragedy.* Oxford: Oxford University Press, 1979.

———. *Conditions Handsome and Unhandsome: Emerson's Constitution of Perfectionism.* Chicago: University of Chicago Press, 1990.

———. *In Quest of the Ordinary: Lines of Skepticism and Romanticism.* Chicago: University of Chicago Press, 1988.

———. *Themes Out of School: Effects and Causes.* San Francisco: North Point Press, 1988.

———. *This New Yet Unapproachable America: Lectures after Emerson after Wittgenstein.* Albuquerque: Living Batch Press, 1989.

Coleridge, Samuel Taylor. *Aids to Reflection.* New York: Chelsea House, 1983.

Crites, Stephen. "The Spacial Dimensions of Narrative Truthtelling." In *Scriptural Authority and Narrative Interpretation.* Edited by Garrett Green. Philadelphia: Fortress Press, 1987.

Davidson, Donald. "On the Very Idea of a Conceptual Scheme." In *Inquiries into Truth and Interpretation.* Oxford: Clarendon Press, 1984.

Demos, Raphael. "Lying to Oneself." *Journal of Philosophy* 57 (1960).

Descartes, René. *Selected Philosophical Writings.* Translated by John Cottingham, Robert Stoothoff, and Dugald Murdoch. Cambridge: Cambridge University Press, 1988.

De Sousa, Ronald. *The Rationality of Emotion.* Cambridge: MIT Press, 1987.

Deutscher, Max. *Subjecting and Objecting.* London: Basil Blackwell, 1983.

Dickinson, Emily. *The Complete Poems of Emily Dickinson.* Edited by Thomas H. Johnson. Boston: Little Brown and Company, 1960.

Dilman, Ilham, and D. Z. Phillips. *Sense and Delusion.* Atlantic Highlands: Humanities Press, 1971.

Dostoyevski, Fyodor. *The Brothers Karamazov.* Translated by Constance Garnett. Revised and edited by Ralph E. Matlaw. New York: W. W. Norton, 1976.

Elster, Jon. *Sour Grapes: Studies in the Subversion of Rationality.* Cambridge: Cambridge University Press, 1983.

———. *Ulysses and the Sirens: Studies in Rationality and Irrationality.* Cambridge: Cambridge University Press, 1984.

Emerson, Ralph Waldo. *The Essays of Ralph Waldo Emerson*. Introduction by Alfred Kazin. Cambridge: Belknap Press, 1987.

————. *Nature, Addresses, and Lectures*. Introduction by Robert E. Spiller. Cambridge: Harvard University Press, 1979

————. *Selections from Ralph Waldo Emerson*. Edited by Stephen E. Whicher. Boston: Houghton Mifflin Company, 1957.

Ferreira, M. Jamie. *Doubt and Religious Commitment: The Role of the Will in Newman's Thought*. Oxford: Clarendon Press, 1980.

Fingarette, Herbert. *Self-Deception*. Atlantic Highlands: Humanities Press, 1969.

Foley, Richard. *The Epistemic Theory of Rationality*. Cambridge: Harvard University Press, 1987.

Frankfurt, Harry. "Freedom of the Will and the Concept of the Person." In *The Importance of What We Care About: Philosophical Essays*. Cambridge: Cambridge University Press, 1988.

Frei, Hans W. *The Eclipse of Biblical Narrative: A Study in Eighteenth and Nineteenth Century Hermeneutics*. New Haven: Yale University Press, 1975.

Green, Garrett. " 'The Bible As . . .' Fictional Narrative and Scriptural Truth." In *Scriptural Authority and Narrative Interpretation*. Edited by Garrett Green. Philadelphia: Fortress Press, 1987.

Gutting, Gary. *Religious Belief and Religious Skepticism*. Notre Dame: University of Notre Dame Press, 1982.

Haight, M. R. *A Study of Self-Deception*. Atlantic Highlands: Humanities Press, 1980.

Hamlyn, D. W. "Self-Knowledge." In *Perception, Learning, and the Self: Essays in the Philosophy of Psychology*. London: Routledge and Kegan Paul, 1983.

Hanfling, Oswald. *The Quest for Meaning*. Oxford: Basil Blackwell, 1988.

Hazlitt, William. *Literary Remains*. New York: Chelsea House, 1983.

Hume, David. *An Inquiry Concerning the Principles of Morals*. Indianapolis: Hackett Publishing, 1983.

Kekes, John. *The Examined Life*. Lewisburg: Bucknell University Press, 1988.

Kenny, Anthony. *The God of the Philosophers*. Oxford: Clarendon Press, 1979.

Kierkegaard, Søren. *Concluding Unscientific Postscript*. Translated by David Swenson and Walter Lowrie. Princeton: Princeton University Press, 1941.

————. *For Self-Examination and Judge for Yourselves!* Translated and introduced by Walter Lowrie. Princeton: Princeton University Press, 1944.

————. *Purity of Heart Is to Will One Thing*. Translated by Douglas V. Steere. New York: Harper and Row, 1956.

————. *The Sickness unto Death*. Edited and translated by Howard and Edna Hong. Princeton: Princeton University Press, 1980.

Kuhn, Thomas. *The Structure of Scientific Revolutions*. Chicago: University of Chicago Press, 1970.

Kuklick, Bruce. *Churchmen and Philosophers from Jonathan Edwards to John Dewey*. New Haven: Yale University Press, 1985.

Lindbeck, George. *The Nature of Doctrine: Religion and Theology in a Postliberal Age*. Philadelphia: The Westminster Press, 1984.

Locke, John. *An Essay Concerning Human Understanding*. Edited and introduced by Peter H. Nidditch. Oxford: Clarendon Press, 1979.

Luckhardt, C. G., ed. *Wittgenstein: Sources and Perspectives*. Sussex: Harvester Press, 1979.

MacIntyre, Alasdair. *After Virtue*. 2d ed. Notre Dame: University of Notre Dame Press, 1984.

————. "The Idea of a Social Science." In *Rationality*. Edited by Bryan R. Wilson. Oxford: Basil Blackwell, 1970.

Mackie, J. L. *The Miracle of Theism*. Oxford: Clarendon Press, 1982.

McLaughlin, Brian P., and Amelie Oksenberg Rorty, eds. *Perspectives on Self-Deception*. Berkeley: University of California Press, 1988.

Martin, Mike. *Self-Deception and Morality*. Lawrence: University of Kansas Press, 1986.

————, ed. *Self-Deception and Self-Understanding: New Essays in Philosophy and Psychology*. Lawrence: University of Kansas Press, 1985.

Mochulsky, Konstantin. *Dostoevsky: His Life and Work.* Translated by Michael A. Minihan. Princeton: Princeton University Press, 1971.

Monk, Ray. *Ludwig Wittgenstein: The Duty of Genius.* New York: The Free Press, 1990.

Nehamas, Alexander. *Nietzsche: Life as Literature.* Cambridge: Harvard University Press, 1985.

Newman, John Henry. *An Essay in Aid of a Grammar of Assent.* Introduction by Nicholas Lash. Notre Dame: University of Notre Dame Press, 1979.

Nielsen, Kai. *An Introduction to the Philosophy of Religion.* New York: St. Martin's Press, 1982.

Nietzsche, Friedrich. *Daybreak: Thoughts on the Prejudices of Morality.* Translated by R. J. Hollingdale. Cambridge: Cambridge University Press, 1982.

———. *The Gay Science.* Translated by Walter Kaufmann. New York: Viking Press, 1974.

———. *Human, All Too Human: A Book for Free Spirits.* Translated by R. J. Hollingdale. Introduction by Erich Heller. Cambridge: Cambridge University Press, 1986.

Nozick, Robert. *The Examined Life: Philosophical Meditations.* New York: Simon and Schuster, 1989.

Nussbaum, Martha. *The Fragility of Goodness: Luck and Ethics in Greek Tragedy and Philosophy.* Cambridge: Cambridge University Press, 1986.

———. *Love's Knowledge: Essays on Philosophy and Literature.* New York: Oxford University Press, 1990.

Passmore, John. "Locke and the Ethics of Belief." In *Rationalism, Empiricism, and Idealism.* Edited by Anthony Kenny. Oxford: Clarendon Press, 1986.

Pears, David. *Motivated Irrationality.* New York: Oxford University Press, 1984.

Phillips, D. Z. *Belief, Change & Forms of Life.* Atlantic Highlands: Humanities Press, 1986.

———. *The Concept of Prayer.* New York: Seabury Press, 1981.

———. *Faith and Philosophical Inquiry*. London: Routledge and Kegan Paul, 1970.

———. *Religion without Explanation*. Oxford: Basil Blackwell, 1976.

Plantinga, Alvin. *God, Freedom, and Evil*. Grand Rapids: William B. Eerdman, 1977.

———. *The Nature of Necessity*. Oxford: Clarendon Press, 1974.

———. "Reason and Belief in God." In *Faith and Rationality: Reason and Belief in God*. Notre Dame: University of Notre Dame Press, 1983.

Pojman, Louis P. *Religious Belief and the Will*. London: Routledge and Kegan Paul, 1986.

Polanyi, Michael. *Personal Knowledge*. Chicago: University of Chicago Press, 1962.

Popkin, Richard. *The History of Scepticism from Erasmus to Spinoza*. Berkeley: University of California Press, 1979.

Proudfoot, Wayne. *Religious Experience*. Berkeley: University of California Press, 1985.

Rhees, Rush, ed. *Recollections of Wittgenstein*. New York: Oxford University Press, 1984.

Rorty, Amelie Oksenberg. "Self-Deception, Akrasia, and Irrationality." In *The Multiple Self*. Edited by Jon Elster. Cambridge: Cambridge University Press, 1987.

Rorty, Richard. *Contingency, Irony and Solidarity*. Cambridge: Cambridge University Press, 1989.

———. *Philosophy and the Mirror of Nature*. Princeton: Princeton University Press, 1979.

Schopenhauer, Arthur. *Parerga and Paralipomena*. 2 Vols. Translated by E. F. J. Payne. Oxford: Clarendon Press, 1974.

———. *The World as Will and Representation*. 2 Vols. Translated by E. F. J. Payne. New York: Dover Books, 1966.

Sherry, Patrick. *Religion, Truth, and Language-Games*. New York: Barnes and Noble, 1977.

Stevenson, C. L. *Ethics and Language*. New Haven: Yale University Press, 1945.

Stout, Jeffrey. *Ethics after Babel: The Languages of Morals and Their Discontents.* Boston: Beacon Press, 1988.

Sutherland, Stewart. *Atheism and the Rejection of God.* Oxford: Basil Blackwell, 1977.

Taylor, Charles. "Self-Interpreting Animals." In *Human Agency and Language: Philosophical Papers I.* London: Cambridge University Press, 1985.

Taylor, Richard. *Good and Evil: A New Direction.* London: Macmillan Company.

Tolstoy, Leo. *Anna Karenina.* Translated by Constance Garnett. Indianapolis: Bobbs-Merrill, 1978.

Van Leer, David. *Emerson's Epistemology.* Cambridge: Cambridge University Press, 1987.

Weil, Simone. *Gravity and Grace.* Translated by Emma Craufurd. London: Ark Paperbacks, 1987.

———. *The Simone Weil Reader.* Edited by George A. Panichas. New York: David McKay Company, 1977.

———. *Waiting for God.* Translated by Emma Craufurd. London: Routledge and Kegan Paul, 1979.

Welch, Claude. "Samuel Taylor Coleridge." In *Nineteenth Century Religious Thought.* Vol. 2. Edited by Ninian Smart, John Clayton, Steven T. Katz, and Patrick Sherry. Cambridge: Cambridge University Press, 1985.

West, Cornel. *The American Evasion of Philosophy.* Madison: University of Wisconsin Press, 1989.

Whicher, Stephen. *Freedom and Fate: An Inner Life of Ralph Waldo Emerson.* Philadelphia: University of Pennsylvania Press, 1953.

Wiggins, David. *Needs, Values, Truth.* Oxford: Basil Blackwell, 1987.

Willey, Basil. *Samuel Taylor Coleridge.* New York: W. W. Norton, 1973.

Williams, Bernard. *Ethics and the Limits of Philosophy.* Cambridge: Harvard University Press, 1985.

———. *Moral Luck: Philosophical Papers 1973–1980.* Cambridge: Cambridge University Press, 1981.

Winch, Peter. *The Idea of a Social Science.* London: Routledge and Kegan Paul, 1958.

————. "Understanding a Primitive Society." In *Rationality*. Edited by Bryan R. Wilson. Oxford: Basil Blackwell, 1970.

Wisdo, David. "Kierkegaard and Euthyphro." *Philosophy* (April 1987).

Wittgenstein, Ludwig. *Culture and Value*. Edited by G. H. von Wright. Translated by Peter Winch. Chicago: University of Chicago Press, 1977.

————. *Lectures and Conversations on Aesthetics, Psychology, and Religious Belief*. Edited by Cyril Barrett. Berkeley: University of California Press, 1968.

————. *Notebooks 1914–1916*. 2d ed. Translated by G. E. M. Anscombe. Chicago: University of Chicago Press, 1979.

————. *Philosophical Investigations*. 3d ed. Translated by G. E. M. Anscombe. New York: Macmillan Company, 1958.

————. "Remarks on Frazer's *The Golden Bough*." In *Wittgenstein: Sources and Perspectives*. Edited by C. G. Luckhardt. Sussex: The Harvester Press, 1979.

————. *Tractatus Logico-Philosophicus*. Translated by D. F. Pears and B. F. McGuinness. London: Routledge and Kegan Paul, 1972.

Yolton, John W. *Locke and the Way of Ideas*. Oxford: Oxford University Press, 1956.

Index

After Virtue (MacIntyre), 19
Aids to Reflection (Coleridge), 24–25, 27, 35 n.20
Allen, Woody, 37
"American Scholar" (Emerson), 2
Anna Karenina (Tolstoy), 6, 39, 56–61, 84, 87, 128
Anscombe, Elizabeth, 113
Aristotle, 31–32; *Nichomachean Ethics*, 31
Attention, virtue of, 8–9, 98–101
Augustine, St., 57

Baier, Annette, 126 n.23
Barth, J. Robert, 25
Barth, Karl, 126 n.21
Beehler, Roger, 126 n.23
Belief, ethics of: basic questions of, 127, 134; of Coleridge, 5, 24–29; of Descartes, 14–16; of Emerson, 1–4; as epistemological concern, 4, 5, 9, 13–14, 16, 22–24, 62, 129; of Kierkegaard, 62–67, 78–80; literary exploration of, 6, 50–51, 54 n.29, 56–57, 62–63, 73–74; of Locke, 4–5, 17–24; and meaning of life, 5–6, 10, 37–51; of Newman, 5, 29–33; of Nietzsche, 67–70, 90–91; as question of personal knowledge, 14–33; as question of self-reflection, 5, 57, 61, 67, 69; and reductionism, 119–124; and self-deception, 73–85; of Wittgenstein, 5, 39–46, 47, 48, 49
Belief, religious: justification of, 1–10, 13–33, 38, 39, 75, 81–85, 88–90, 118,

127–128; and self-understanding, 5, 6, 55–70; truth of, 38, 39
Bergman, Ingmar, 74, 81, 82, 84, 85, 87, 128; *Winter Light*, 74, 82–85, 87
Bradley, Stephen, 116–117
Brothers Karamazov (Dostoyevski), 73, 94–97, 99
Bushnell, Horace, 35 n.20

Cameron, J. M., 36 n.32
Camus, Albert, 47, 100, 103 n.24
Cavell, Stanley, 24, 56, 107
"Circles" (Emerson), 134–135
Clifford, W. K., 127
Coleridge, Samuel Taylor, 32, 35 n.20, 55, 75, 127–128; *Aids to Reflection*, 24–25, 27, 35 n.20; ethics of belief of, 5, 24–29
Contingency, Irony and Solidarity (R. Rorty), 137
Crites, Stephen, 51

Davidson, Donald, 106, 113, 125 n.10
Daybreak (Nietzsche), 67–68
Death of Ivan Ilych (Tolstoy), 73
Descartes, Rene, 4; *Discourse on Method*, 14; ethics of belief of, 14–16
DeSousa, Ronald, 139 n.4
Deutscher, Max, 130–134
Dewey, John, 137
Dickinson, Emily, 105
Discourse on Method (Descartes), 14
Divided self, 77, 79
Dostoyevski, Fyodor, 8, 73, 94, 102 n.17, 137; *Brothers Karamazov*, 73, 94–97, 99

Doubt, 82–85
Doubt and Religious Commitment:
The Role of Will in Newman's
Thought (Ferreira), 36 n.32
Durkheim, Emile, 115

Eclipse of Biblical Narrative (Frei), 50
Edification, 14, 27–28, 31
Edwards, Jonathan: Religious Affec-
tions, 81
Either/Or (Kierkegaard), 63
Eliade, Mircea, 122
Elster, Jon, 76
Emerson, Ralph Waldo, 35 n.20, 139
n.13; "American Scholar," 2;
"Circles," 134–135; and ethics of
belief, 1–4; "Experience," 135–136;
and pragmatism, 9–10, 10–11 n.2,
134–138
Emersonian pragmatism, 134–138
Emotion, James-Lange theory of, 116
Emotivism, 39–40
Epistemology, 20, 21, 106, 107;
Christian, 27–28, 128, 137–138;
empiricist, 29–30; ethics of belief as
concern of, 4, 5, 9, 13–14, 16, 22–24,
62, 129; reformed, 7, 88–92, 129;
romantic, 121–122, 126 n.21
Essay Concerning Human Under-
standing (Locke), 4, 17, 28, 34 n.8
Essay in Aid of a Grammar of Assent
(Newman), 29
Ethics of belief. See Belief, ethics of
Euthyphro question, 52 n.10
Evans-Pritchard, E. E., 111–112
Evidentialism, 17, 88
Evil, problem of, 7–9, 92–97, 98–101,
129
Existential facts, 38, 39
"Experience" (Emerson), 135–136
Experimentalism, 67–68

Fact, distinction between value and,
41–42, 44, 45–46, 47

Faith: fragility of, 9, 51, 87–101, 129,
136; loss of, 87, 92–97, 100–101,
136–137
Fallibilism, 90, 93
Fear and Trembling (Kierkegaard),
79–80
Ferreira, M. Jamie, 36 n.32
Fideism, Wittgensteinian, 42, 46, 52
n.10, 53 n. 14, 111
Flew, Anthony, 92, 127
Foundationalism, 88–90
Fragility of faith, 9, 51, 87–101, 129, 136
Frankfurt, Harry, 75–76, 97
Frazer, James, 109, 110, 119–120, 122,
129
Free Will Defense, 93–96, 129
Frei, Hans, 50
Freud, Sigmund, 109, 110–111, 127

Gay Science (Nietzsche), 91
Geertz, Clifford, 114
Geneology of Morals (Nietzsche), 69
God, existence of, 21–23, 81, 83–84,
88–90, 93
God, Freedom, and Evil (Plantinga), 93
Grand Inquisitor (Brothers
Karamazov), 95, 97
Gravity and Grace (Weil), 98–99
Green, Garrett, 51

Hamlyn, D. W., 61–62
Hardy, Thomas, 73
Hare, R. M., 47
Hartley, David, 25
Hazlitt, William, 13
Hegel, G. W. F., 66
Heidegger, Martin, 4
History of Scepticism from Erasmus
to Spinoza (Popkin), 15
Homo religiosus, 122
Human, All Too Human (Nietzsche),
74
Hume, David, 30, 36 n.32, 108, 109,
123, 126 n.23, 127; Natural History
of Religion, 109

Ibsen, Henrik, 74
Idea of a Social Science (Winch), 111
Illative sense, 30, 31–32
Irony, 74–75, 80

James, William, 44, 45, 137; *Varieties of Religious Experience*, 116
Jaspers, Karl, 58
Jude the Obscure (Hardy), 73
Judge for Yourselves! (Kierkegaard), 65

Karamazov, Aloysha (*Brothers Karamazov*), 95, 96, 97
Karamazov, Ivan (*Brothers Karamazov*), 7, 8, 94–101, 102 n.17, 103 n.24, 129, 137
Kenny, Anthony, 94
Kierkegaard, Søren, 1, 4, 6, 25, 27, 29, 45, 52 n.10, 55, 68, 74, 128, 134, 135, 136, 137; *Either/Or*, 63; *Fear and Trembling*, 79–80; *Judge for Yourselves!*, 65; *Purity of Heart*, 64; on self-deception, 78–80; on self-knowledge, 62–67; *Sickness Unto Death*, 63–64, 81; on subjectivity, 62, 99
Knowledge, personal, 14–33, 127–128
Knowledge, religious, 24–26, 29. *See also* Belief, religious; Belief, ethics of

Language, Wittgenstein on, 42–43, 46, 49
"Lectures on Religious Belief" (Wittgenstein), 43
Lessing, Gotthold, 138
Levin, Konstantin (*Anna Karenina*), 57–61, 84, 87, 128
Life, meaning of, 55–56, 69–70, 87, 96, 97, 128, 129–130; and ethics of belief, 5–6, 10, 37–51; literary exploration of, 50–51, 54 n.29; Wiggins on, 46–51; Wittgenstein on, 52 n.10
Lindbeck, George, 126 n.21

Literature: exploration of meaning of life through, 50–51, 54 n.29; exploration of ethics of belief through, 6, 50–51, 54 n.29, 56–57, 62–63, 73–74
Locke, John, 7, 25, 30, 34 n.8, 36 n.32, 55, 75, 88, 92, 127, 134; *Essay Concerning Human Understanding*, 4, 17, 29, 34 n.8; ethics of belief of, 4–5, 17–24; and religious enthusiasm, 19, 20, 21, 24, 29, 31, 34 n.8; on subjective interests, 28–29

MacIntyre, Alasdair, 19, 34 n.12, 40, 50, 111, 112; *After Virtue*, 19
Mackie, J. L., 94
Marsh, James, 35 n.20
Marx, Karl, 127
Master Builder (Ibsen), 74
Meaning, picture-theory of, 41–42, 44, 46, 49
Meaning of life. *See* Life, meaning of
Mochulsky, Konstantin, 102 n.17
Montaigne, Michel de, 16
More, Henry, 28
Murdoch, Iris, 50

Nagel, Thomas, 47
Narrative, 50–51
Natural History of Religion (Hume), 109
Nature of Necessity (Plantinga), 93
Newman, John Henry, 24, 35 n.20, 36 n.32, 75, 127–128; *Essay in Aid of a Grammar of Assent*, 29; ethics of belief of, 5, 29–33; on illative sense, 30, 31–32
Nichomachean Ethics (Aristotle), 31
Nielsen, Kai, 52 n.10, 53 n.14
Nietzsche, Friedrich, 2, 57, 115, 127, 134, 136; *Daybreak*, 67, 68; ethics of belief of, 67–70, 90–91; *Gay Science*, 91; *Geneology of Morals*, 69; *Human, All Too Human*, 74; on self-deception, 74–75, 77, 78

Noncognitivism, 46–49
Notebooks, 1914–1916 (Wittgenstein), 40, 41, 44, 47
Nussbaum, Martha, 50, 54 n.29, 56

Objectivity, 112; vs. subjectivity, 9–10, 13–33, 38, 39, 130–134
On Certainty (Wittgenstein), 36 n.32, 118
Otto, Rudolph, 121–122

Pascal, Blaise, 30, 80
Passmore, J. A., 20, 34 n.8
Personal knowledge, 14–33, 127–128
Personal Knowledge (Polanyi), 35 n.18
"Persons, Character, and Morality" (Williams), 68
Phillips, D. Z., 9, 52–53 n.14, 106, 107–111, 111, 112, 113, 115, 119, 123–124, 129; Religion Without Explanation, 108
Philosophical Investigations (Wittgenstein), 44, 123
Philosophy and the Mirror of Nature (A. Rorty), 137
Picture-theory of meaning, 41–42, 44, 46, 49
Plain truth, 48–51, 53–54 n.25, 128
Plantinga, Alvin, 7, 8, 98, 101, 129; on evil, 93–96; God, Freedom and Evil, 93; Nature of Necessity, 93; "Reason and Belief in God," 88; on reformed epistemology, 88–92
Pojman, Louis P., 36 n.32
Polanyi, Michael, 23, 35 n.18, 127
Popkin, Richard, 15–16
Pragmatism, Emersonian, 134–138
Priestley, Joseph, 25
Proudfoot, Wayne, 9, 106–107, 113–118, 119, 123, 126 n.21, 129; Religious Experience, 113
Purity of Heart (Kierkegaard), 64

Rationality, 9, 10, 76, 88, 105, 106, 108, 109, 113

Rawls, John, 19
"Reason and Belief in God" (Plantinga), 88
Reductionism, 96–97, 129, 134; case against, 107–113; descriptive vs. explanatory, 113–118; worries about, 105–107
Relativism, 106, 111, 112–113, 125 n.10
Religion: as cultural tradition, 37–38, 111–112, 119–123, 124; romantic, 125–126 n.21; social scientific approach to, 108, 110–111, 113–118, 119–120, 122
Religion Without Explanation (Phillips), 108
Religious Affections (Edwards), 81
Religious belief. See Belief, religious
Religious Experience (Proudfoot), 113
"Remarks on Frazer's The Golden Bough" (Wittgenstein), 9, 119
Rorty, Amelie, 76–78
Rorty, Richard, 137–138

Sartre, Jean-Paul, 47, 74
Schachter, Stanley, 116
Schleiermacher, Friedrich, 121–122
Schopenhauer, Arthur, 37, 39, 40, 41, 47, 74, 127
Self-deception, 6–7, 56, 57, 65, 70, 87, 95, 102 n.17, 128; and ethics of belief, 73–85
Self-interpretation, 65, 91, 92, 97, 135
Self-reflection, 57, 61, 65, 67, 68, 69, 129
Self-trust, 1–4, 9–10
Self-understanding, 5, 6, 136, 138; and religious belief, 55–70
Sextus Empiricus, 16
Sherry, Patrick, 53 n.14
Shtcherbatskaya, Kitty (Anna Karenina), 57–60
Sickness Unto Death (Kierkegaard), 63, 81
Sin, 7, 26–27, 63, 79

Skepticism, 16, 21, 57, 67, 68, 118, 131, 132, 134
Social scientific approach to religion, 108, 110–111, 113–118, 119–120, 122
Spinoza, Benedict, 109
Stephen, Leslie, 127
Stout, Jeffrey, 19, 34 n.8, 125 n.10
Subjecting and Objecting (Deutscher), 131
Subjectivity, 69, 99; vs. objectivity, 9–10, 13–33, 38, 39, 130–134; truth as, 62
Suffering, 92–97
Sutherland, Stewart, 97, 100, 102–103 n.20, 103 n.24

Taylor, Charles, 91, 92
Taylor, Richard, 47
Theologico-Political Treatise (Spinoza), 109
Tolstoy, Leo, 41, 128; *Anna Karenina*, 6, 39, 56–61, 84, 87; *Death of Ivan Ilych*, 73
Toulmin, Stephen, 36 n.32
Tractatus Logico-Philosophicus (Wittgenstein), 40, 41, 42, 44, 47, 49
Trainor, Kevin, 126 n.27
Truth, 27, 74, 75; life as apprenticeship to, 135–138; plain, 48–51, 53–54 n.25, 128; of religious beliefs, 38, 39; search for, 17–18, 20–21, 28–29; as subjectivity, 62
"Truth, Invention and the Meaning of Life" (Wiggins), 46
Tylor, E. B., 109, 110

Underdetermination, doctrine of cognitive, 48–51
"Understanding and Primitive Society" (Winch), 111–112

Value, distinction between fact and, 41–42, 44, 45–46, 47
Van Leer, David, 139 n.13

Varieties of Religious Experience (James), 116
Vice, 21, 133–134
Virtue of attention, 8–9, 98–101
Volitionalism, 47, 49, 75, 98

Wagner, Richard, 74
Weber, Max, 115
Weil, Simone, 84, 88, 103 n.24, 129; on affliction, 87; *Gravity and Grace*, 98–99; on problem of evil, 8–9, 97–101
Wiggins, David, 5, 39, 53–54 n.25, 128; on meaning of life, 46–51; "Truth, Invention and the Meaning of Life," 46
Williams, Bernard, 68–69, 93
Wilson, Cook, 109
Winch, Peter, 9, 106, 107, 111–113, 115, 119, 123, 124; *Idea of a Social Science*, 111; "Understanding a Primitive Society," 111–112
Winter Light (Bergman), 74, 82–85, 87
Wisdom, John, 36 n.32
Wittgenstein, Ludwig, 24, 29, 51, 55, 56, 61, 99, 100, 108, 111, 126 nn.21, 23, 128; on doubt, 118; ethics of belief of, 5, 39–46, 47, 48, 49; on fact-value distinction, 41–42, 44, 45–46, 47; on language, 42–43, 46, 49; "Lectures on Religious Belief," 43; on meaning of life, 52 n.10; *Notebooks, 1914–1916*, 40, 41, 44, 47; *On Certainty*, 36 n.32, 118; *Philosophical Investigations*, 44, 123; picture-theory of meaning of, 41–42, 44, 46, 49; and reductionism, 9, 106, 107, 119–123, 129; "Remarks on Frazer's *The Golden Bough*," 9, 119; on the self, 76; on self-deception, 73; *Tractatus Logico-Philosophicus*, 40, 41, 42, 44, 47, 49
Wittgensteinian fideism, 42, 46, 52 n.10, 53 n.14, 111